DEVON'S
TESTIMONY OF

A COLLECTION OF PERSONAL
REMINISCENCES OF THE SECOND WORLD WAR

Edited and compiled by
IAN MAXTED

DEVON BOOKS

First published in Great Britain in 1995 by Devon Books

British Library Cataloguing in Publication Data

Data for this publication is available from the British Library

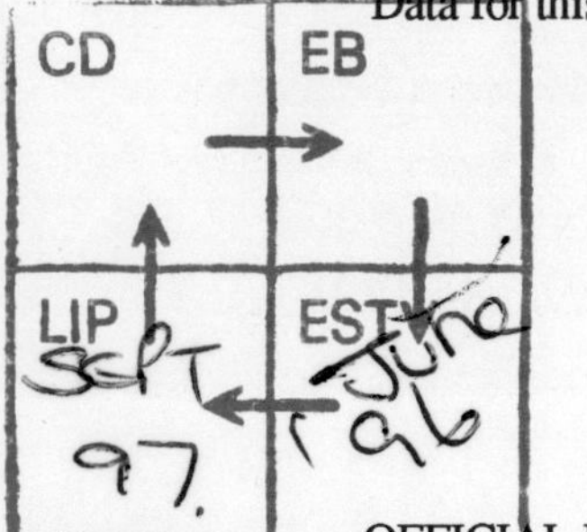

ISBN 0 86114 892 4

DEVON BOOKS
OFFICIAL PUBLISHER TO DEVON COUNTY COUNCIL

Halsgrove House
Lower Moor Way
Tiverton, Devon EX16 6SS
Tel: 01884 243242
Fax: 01884 243325

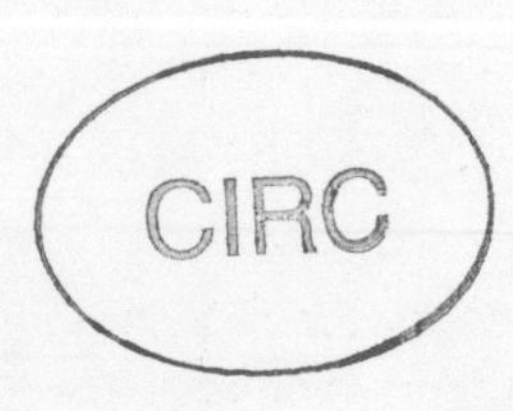

Printed in Great Britain by Culm Print, Tiverton

The cover illustrstions are taken from contemporary wartime illustrations

INTRODUCTION

As part of Devon County Council's commemoration of the fiftieth anniversary of the D-Day landings it was decided to appeal to Devonians to submit reminiscences of their experiences during the Second World War, whether in the armed services or on the home front. Almost one hundred individuals replied and the result is a rich and frequently moving eye-witness account of a period in Devon's history which rivals in importance such events as the Spanish Armada or the Civil War.

The testimonies vary widely in both style and content, from memories of everyday problems, such as buying a dress to graphic accounts of what it was like to take part in the Normandy landings. Some people have had to struggle against arthritis or other disabilities to commit their memories to paper - all have felt that it is important that others can learn from their experiences. For this reason the individual testimonies included here have normally been transcribed in their entirety. Only where they are lengthy and a minority is relevant to Devon have sections been omitted and this is clearly indicated in the text. In these cases, and in the cases of testimonies which have not been included in this publication, the full texts can be seen in the Westcountry Studies Library in Exeter. At times small amendments have been made to standardise presentation and for the sake of clarity. It has not proved possible to verify all the events mentioned in the testimony. An important general book which can help in this is *Devon at War* by Gerald Wasley (Devon Books 1994).

Because many testimonies cover a variety of topics they have been listed in alphabetical order with an index of subjects. Unfortunately not all the material collected could appear in this small book. An extended selection is available on audio tape from Westcountry Books, Halsgrove House, Lower Moor Way, Tiverton Devon EX16 6SS.

The book concludes with a short piece from a Jewish exile who escaped from Vienna just before the war to live in Exeter. This extract is taken from reminiscences collected by Frank Gent and Lucy MacKeith as part of an exhibition *Anne Frank in the World* held in Exeter Cathedral in 1989.

Ian Maxted
County Local Studies Librarian

LIST OF CONTRIBUTORS

Mrs J. M. Almond
Mrs Gerald Barker
Mr D.H. Berry
Mrs J.M. Bishop
R. B. Blatchford MBE
Mrs Greta E. Bray
Mr D.W. Brush
Dr Ronald Cox
Mrs E. Curtis
Mrs Mavis Danks
Mrs J. Dubicki-Matthews
Peter Fletcher
Mrs Barbara Halls
Mr Bert Hitchen
Mr J. Holwell
Miss A.G. Illingworth
Mr R. Jackson
Mr R. C. Johns
Mrs D. Joint
Mr R. Kneebone
Mrs M. Lawrence
Mrs P. A. Merrett
Mr J. T. Newton
Mrs E. Patterson
Mrs P. D. Reeve
Mr H. R. RiceJr
Mr R. Smith
Mr M. Swain
Mr T. Trevail
Mrs V. Vincent
Col. David Wood MBE
Mr Kurt Wilhelm

GOD IS OUR REFUGE...

MRS J.M. ALMOND (Living in Braunton, 1941)

I was born and bred in Braunton, as the saying goes, also my mother was born in Braunton, belonging to the Lamprey family. My father was Spanish, living in Braunton from the age of 30 years until he died aged 78. [Mr & Mrs J.Gutierrez lived at 1, Kings End, Station Road, Braunton.].

When Chivenor opened the police came round to the houses in Braunton to see if there were any spare bedrooms to put up airmen until Chivenor erected huts for them. The people got paid for bed and breakfast for the airmen they used to billet, two airmen to each bedroom. The airmen became a part of the family and my Mum used to do all the airmen's washing for them. One of the pairs of airmen that stayed with us was called Jimmy, a Yorkshire lad. He was on duty one night in 1941 when a German plane actually landed at Chivenor. It tried to take off again but the ground staff, Jimmy being one of them, stopped it from taking off and the German crew were taken to Barnstaple police station. The German plane had thought that the Bristol Channel was the English Channel, so thought they were landing in France. It seems that Chivenor were using the same lights as their code. Jimmy came home early in the morning, had his breakfast and went to bed without saying a word about this. Mum went up to Ellis the butcher in South Street and the commanding officer was in the shop and said to Mum, "I bet you are proud of your lad Jimmy, Mrs Gutierrez." You see Braunton was small then and everybody knew everybody else. Of course, Mum didn't half tell Jimmy off when he got down from bed. I was at school and heard about the German plane and the next day I went to school I was ten feet high because it was our Jimmy that helped catch the Germans and the plane.

There used to be a German prisoner of war camp at Saunton Golf Club. As kids we used to cycle to Saunton, pushing our bikes up the hill. The really bad prisoners used to exercise in a barbed wired piece of ground right beside the hill. Our soldiers were on guard with guns and the prisoners used to look at us with terrible looks. The good German prisoners used to wear a light blue round patch on the back of their overalls because they were allowed into Braunton shopping, and some worked for local farmers. I used to go to the Methodist Chapel in Hills View and our minister, the Rev. Biggin, was the Germans' chaplain and on Sunday evenings the good Germans were brought to the Chapel by army truck and they attended our evening service. After the service they went into the school room and had tea, cakes and sandwiches. We used to help out serving them. Some were old and some were very young. One Christmas they all stood up in Chapel and sang "Silent night" in German. They sang it so beautifully that whenever I hear it I remember that time. I think nearly everyone had a tear in their eye, I know my Mum and Dad and I did.

I was at Braunton Junior School, Caen Street through the War and I have a memory of when the siren went because of German planes in the area. We all - girls, boys, teachers - went into concrete air raid shelters built in the school yard. Of course everyone had their gas masks; you carried them everywhere, even took them to bed. One of the teachers taught us a poem to say, and I have never forgotten it. You see, Chivenor would send up their planes and you would also hear a German plane. It had a sort of droning noise different from our planes. So, being very young and frightened, we all used to say this as a prayer:

God is our refuge, be not afraid

He will take care of us all through the raid.

When bombs are dropping and danger is near

He will be with us until the all-clear.

Do you know, it made us feel better.

My Mum was in the St John's Ambulance and my Dad in the Home Guard. The parish hall in Braunton was a first aid centre during the War. It was all fitted out with beds etc and when my Mum and my Dad were both on duty, I used to be taken up to the parish hall and put to bed. We had an evacuee, a girl, with us from London for a while during the War. The children from London were brought to Braunton by train and taken to Fortesue House, Wrafton Road, where the people who had agreed to take them went and fetched them. The St John's Ambulance were there because some of the children had been in dug-outs (air raid shelters) and were in a terrible state with fleas in their hair and an awful lot of scabies, a skin complaint, because of living underground in poor conditions, and of course London had terrible bombing.

Saunton Sands Hotel was taken over during the War for the Duke of York boys from Dover. They were all sons of army men. Some of their dads had been killed, and the army placed them in this school. They all wore army uniforms and every Saturday night an army truck would pick up local girls from Braunton and Barnstaple for a dance at the Saunton Sands Hotel. Their ages were from about ten years old to prefects of about seventeen or eighteen.

The Bulb Farm in Sandy Lane, Saunton Road, a flower farm, had one of its fields made into a dummy aerodrome and when Chivenor was night flying they used to light up the dummy aerodrome with the same Very light along a make-believe runway and one night when the Jerries made a raid it bombed the dummy aerodrome and I remember all we kids on bikes went over and saw the great big hole the bomb had made. Of course we could not get too near, they had Air Force military police on duty.

We were lucky in Braunton but we did have some machine-gun bullets in the guttering of some houses in Wrafton and some farm buildings at Wrafton were hit by a bomb. We used to leave our houses because, right or wrong, our parents thought we were better out in the open. I suppose because of Station Road being near the railway, Mum used to say the German planes may follow the railway lines. You see, it always seemed to be moonlight when we had an air-raid. I remember going up the Beacon, a hill overlooking Braunton. A lot of people used to go up there in the open and we could see across to Wales and could see the bombing there.

We had the U.S. Army camp on the Saunton Road. When the troops went away after their training we kids used to go up to Braunton Railway Station and give the troops packets of sandwiches and biscuits which our mothers had packed for them for their journey, and we used to stand on the platform and wave the troops goodbye.

A PLYMOUTH BOY'S ADVENTURE

MR GERALD BARKER (Plymouth)

As a brief respite from the almost nightly air raids on Plymouth, I, together with a group of seven or eight other boys aged 13 or 14 would set off on our bicycles to camp for the weekend at Bickleigh Vale, which lay in a valley near woods on the way to Dartmoor. One lad would remain behind in case a raid on the Friday or Saturday night resulted in an unexploded bomb or worse in the vicinity of one of our houses. If this happened, and it did, the boy whose house was threatened would ride home to give assistance with the removal of furniture.

One night, soon after we had fallen asleep in the white tent that we had erected, our peace was shattered by the sound of a plane diving and machine guns firing, too near for comfort. We scrambled out of the tent in the darkness and after hastily putting on some footwear we dashed for the bridge. We had recently decided that an opening in the side of the concrete structure was intended for explosives to be placed in the event of enemy invasion. I was the last one to squeeze inside. Within seconds the ground outside was lit up by huge flares that must have been dropped by the enemy aircraft. The machine gunning continued so we raced to the cover of an old farm shed which we considered was less of a target.

The following days, after we had returned home to Plymouth, meant taking frequent trips to the air-raid shelter. No matter how heavy the bombing, or how noisy the anti-aircraft guns trying to hit the aircraft among the criss-crossing searchlights, or the sight of tracer bullets soaring skywards; nothing equalled the experience of sitting under the bridge at Bickleigh Vale with the sound of machine gun bullets seemingly trying to hit our tent and the closeness of the bright flares falling almost within touching distance from what we thought was a safe refuge. Much later we found out that a military establishment had been erected in a wooded area of the Vale in about 1941.

INTO NORMANDY

5626449 PTE BERRY D.H. (4th BN, Somerset light Infantry 43rd Wessex Division).

Landed in Normandy on 19 June 1944. We had a very rough crossing; the boat I was in got lost from the convoy. During the night nobody in sight. In the morning everyone was seasick including the sailors. On 25 June we started to move up the line just behind Cheux where we came under shell fire for the first time. On 10 July the Battalion attacked Hill 112, I was in C Company, casualties were heavy all around me. I saw Major Wardle go down wounded and start to dig himself in. During our stay on the hill the Germans counter-attacked and we were nearly overrun. On the second or third night we were relieved and moved to the bottom of the hill into German slit trenches. I was then wounded in the right hand and evacuated to England by hospital ship to Southampton, then on to Dewsbury Hospital. Four months later I returned to C Company thirteen platoon on the Dutch German border. It was bitter cold weather, with deep snow and we were glad to get back to Treebeck in comfortable billets. From there we moved on to Belgium. On our way to the German counter-offensive in the Ardennes, which was halted, we had Christmas dinner in Liege. On 28 January 1945 we returned to Treebeck for regrouping.

On 9-12 February we went to attack Cleve for which we paid a heavy price. The town had taken terrible punishment, hardly a house intact, craters and trees across the roads making them impassable. By 12 February the road out of Cleve was open and the advance continued. Our task was to capture Bedburg. On the way to Goach, about 20 February, the Battalion was ordered to capture the village of Halverboont. It was during this attack I saw the Company Commander, Major Mallalieu get killed. I was about 20 feet away. On 27 February the Battalion moved up to take over from the Canadians in positions overlooking Calcar. On 1 March I was wounded in the left arm and sent back to the Canadian Hospital in Holland. On the 2 March from there I flew from Brussels to Swindon in a Dakota then by train to Derby Hospital.

UNFAMILIAR LANDSCAPE

MRS J.M. BISHOP (Exeter)

I didn't do anything in the Second World War!

Born and brought up in Exeter, I well remember that last week of peace. Our family holiday was usually taken in Cornwall, this time we took day trips to South Devon resorts in the tense atmosphere of those final days.

One day as we walked along the canal tow path near Exeter, we saw a sea-going vessel ready to sail, when a taxi drew up, a man with an attaché case jumped out and quickly boarded the ship, which was soon under way. Who was he? Where was he going? We never discovered!

On the Saturday, we were in Torquay, where a number of Royal Navy ships were at anchor outside the harbour. Already painted battleship grey, the day too was grey and lowering. There was a sudden flurry as sailors made for the Liberty boats, and, as we stood there, an officer raced up in a huge, open tourer. He missed the launch and stood impotently on the quayside. We returned home, very subdued.

Next day, that unforgettable 3 September 1939, we heard Mr Chamberlain announce that we were at war with Nazi Germany. Even at eleven years old I was aware of the gravity of this declaration. My parents had never expected to see another conflict in their lifetime, after the Great War that was to end all wars. The future looked uncertain for us all.

When the first air-raid siren sounded one night, we all trooped downstairs in our dressing gowns. We squatted behind the sofa, well away from the windows (as yet unprotected against breakage). My parents, small brother and I huddled under a table top which we held over our heads! Then the all clear sounded - it was a false alarm.

Some incidents were funny. Of course we laughed at ourselves. In the immortal works of Mrs Mopp of ITMA fame, “It’s being so cheerful as keeps us going”. Popular songs of the time to which we all knew the words, were: “Roll Out the Barrel”, “Run, Rabbit, Run”, “The White Cliffs of Dover” and “We’ll Meet Again”. Old First World War favourites like “Tipperary” also expressed our feelings.

Another night when the warning went, for some reason my father didn’t put the light on to dress. We were in fits of laughter when he appeared downstairs in a black tail-coat - and the most disreputable pair of old grey gardening trousers!

There were terrible times when we heard of heavy losses on land, sea and in the air; of civilian casualties after unremitting bombardment in other cities. Easter 1941 my father was buried alive under rubble during a raid on Bristol. He was badly shocked when rescued later, but uninjured.

Enemy planes frequently crossed Devon skies on the way to bomb targets in South Wales and the Midlands. Later, we’d hear them return as we recognised the distinctive sound of their aircraft.

By 1940 I was in the Royal Devon and Exeter Hospital in Southernhay at the start of a prolonged bout of ill-health. A bone infection took five and a half years to clear. No penicillin available for civilians. I stoically endured several painful operations. If not an in-patient then I regularly - daily - attended for out-patient treatment. I was in the hospital (Newcourt Ward) the night the bomb fell on the adjoining chapel. I remember being sent home early after an operation, as beds were urgently needed for Plymouth blitz victims. Ten days later I was back in for more surgery, which left a life long scar on my face.

After France fell, there were several tip and run raids, both by night and by day. The worst raid was on 3/4 May 1942. A brilliant moonlit night, when all hell broke loose. A Baedeker raid following a RAF strike against Lubeck, as Exeter Cathedral was bombed in reprisal, and the city centre laid waste. My enduring memory is of sitting beside my blind grandfather, who calmly held my hand throughout. Dry-eyed, but numb with fear, I heard the bombs whistle down. Our home and most of our possessions were lost that night.

Next morning, a thick pall of smoke obscured the sky. A foul, sickening stench of burning foodstuffs etc. permeated the atmosphere. The devastation of the lovely old city seemed unreal as my mother took my grandparents, my brother and me to the country to stay with my godmother. It was a nightmare journey. Frequently turned back by ARP wardens because of unexploded bombs, or blocked rubble-strewn roads, we later learnt that we'd driven over undiscovered bombs anyway, thinking our passage safe. It took hours to clear the now unfamiliar landscape.

We left a ravaged city to find it was a lovely, sunny morning. The peace and tranquillity of the village was like a different world.

No gas, no electricity, no water, but, irony of ironies, a Morrison shelter was delivered to our bombed out Exeter home within days of the raid! An unsightly steel "cage" with thick steel top and wire mesh side pieces, it was claustrophobic to sleep in. One tried not to think of being in it if the house collapsed and buried it. We two children spent many nights in it on our return to Exeter. Mercifully, its efficiency was never put to the test.

The Maynard School was damaged, but arrangements were made for us to share Bishop Blackall premises, each school attending for half a day, so that life continued with minimum disruption. No escape there, alas!

No more teas at Dellers ever again. Trips to the coast were curtailed, beach fortifications and the ever present threat of daylight air attacks made them vulnerable. Only towards the end of the war was I allowed to go to the cinema.

Large water tanks and public air-raid shelters were erected in the open areas of the city, and ARP wardens insisted on everyone taking shelter when the siren went. Traders found themselves make-do premises, proudly announcing "Business As Usual". Blackout, rationing, shortages of many items, with Spam sandwiches, dried egg omelettes - but no bananas! The war dragged on until one morning in June 1944.

For weeks we had seen planes towing gliders over Exeter. Men and machines vanished overnight. The Yanks had gone from the nearby billet; there were no more

US troops slouching along the road or hanging around Boots' corner, whistling and catcalling, and no more Jeeps racing around the town. D-Day had finally arrived.

Despite the drabness, the restrictions and the great empty spaces, life went on with renewed hope. We felt that we were winning through. Pleasures were simple. I used to cycle to Topsham, sit on the Goat Walk and revise for School Certificates. My health improved, I went horse riding in Alphington, there were school friends for company (one had been a German refugee girl from pre-war Hamburg). I read a lot, mainly borrowed books, one of my school books was tenth-hand, such was the scarcity of paper products.

New clothes were a rare treat. School uniform took a lot of clothing coupons, and size 5 shoes were very hard to find. I never felt any resentment or bitterness. It was all part of the on-going war effort.

The final horror of the skeletal Belsen victims confronting us from cinema screens left us stunned with disbelief. Man's inhumanity to man was unbounded. Returning Prisoners of War added their witness to further atrocities. I felt only relief, not excitement, when VE then VJ day arrived.

One strong theme ran through all my days. When this is all over, I promised myself, I shall travel and see the world. The travel urge had been there since childhood, and I was always fascinated by places mentioned on the "wireless" as the war moved from sphere to sphere. I survived to live and travel world-wide... but that is another story!

TRAINING FOR WAR

R.B. BLATCHFORD MBE

Conscription was reintroduced for young men, with an option of joining the Territorial Forces to get evening and weekend training, and the Territorial Army was doubled. I was affected by this and, being in the middle of exams, elected to join the 6th Battalion Devonshire Regiment T.A. at Barnstaple Drill Hall - a culture shock as a private being mixed in with all sorts and sizes. The Unit, having been split in two to form the 9th Devons was very short of officers, NCOs, and the only equipment was from the First World War, except for a bren gun carrier (track laying vehicle lightly armoured with a Ford V8 30 h.p. engine from Ford's factory at Dagenham) one bren light machine gun and one three-inch mortar. Our first job was removing the grease from old Lee Enfield rifles stored from World War One. There were only three permanent staff, an adjutant (Major Symons), a regimental sergeant major (R.S.M.Peddar) and a storeman. Headquarters Company was in Barnstaple with rifle companies at South Molton, Torrington, Holsworthy and Bideford. We had to share the Drill Hall with the HQ of a battery of 142 Field Regiment Royal Artillery (North Devon Hussars). As I had knowledge of electricity and magnetism, I was placed in the signal platoon under Sergeant ——, who was a Post Office telegraphist. His morse was terrific but his organisation pathetic. All the equipment was First World War. We had telephone line equipment comprising D3 telephone sets which rarely worked. All calling was done by buzzer and the HQ exchange consisted of a series of receivers on a board, and if something buzzed you covered up the receivers in turn to find out which one was calling and plugged into that. It was all done on earth return so much of the communication had to be by Morse. We also heliographs (OK in India perhaps), signalling lamps and flags. Most messages went by runner or bicycle on manoeuvres. I was usually organising the signal office and was soon promoted to Lance Corporal. I can only remember shooting on the range at Filleigh (five rounds as there was little ammunition) and weekend exercises on Halsinger Down, as being of any benefit, though I suppose we learned to fall in, march and salute.

BALACLAVAS & BOMBERS

GRETA E. BRAY (North Devon)

I can still remember the cold shudder that ran through me as I head those fateful words 'England is at war with Germany' spoken over the air by our then Prime Minister, Neville Chamberlain. It was September 3rd 1939. I was almost fourteen and a half years of age and alone in our house. Looking back, I can still remember the thoughts which raced through my mind. All those stories which I had heard from 'grown-ups' of the 'Great War' as it was then called, rose before me. The 1914-1918 war which people had thought to be 'The war to end all wars'. Those tragic stories seemed almost a part of me. 'The Kaiser' was such a familiar name. I felt as though I had known him. Now a new name had emerged - that of Adolf Hitler.

The changes soon came. Words hitherto almost unknown to us began to enter into our daily conversations. Words such as ration books, clothes-coupons, identity-cards, Home Guard, air-raid precautions, air-raid shelters, black-outs, joined-up, called-up, conscientious objectors, gas masks and evacuees. Train loads of evacuees were now coming to the South West to be compulsorily billeted to those households who had room for them. We did not have any because a few weeks previously my parents had received a pleading letter from an acquaintance asking them to accommodate her daughter and two children who were living in London and whose husband had already been 'called up'. This meant that we already had eight people living in a four-bedroomed house. I can recall some sad stories of children being sent into homes where they were not wanted. There were also happy ones where the children fitted in well and who even today come back and visit their war-time homes.

During this time I was cycling to Barnstaple each day to what was then known as the B.G.G.S. (Barnstaple Girls' Grammar School). The school had had strict rules when wearing uniform out of school. Hats must always be worn and nothing must be eaten in the street. Even this seemed to change. Now the biggest crime we could commit was to arrive at school without our gas-masks. We had many air-raid practices. When the air-raid siren sounded we would leave our work, troop down the path quickly (in an orderly manner of course) and crouch by a wall near the River Taw (East of Rock Path). Fortunately these were only trial runs. We never had any real raids. By this time the school was full to overflowing. This was due to the coming of the evacuees. One of my proudest moments, I recollect, was when I was able to present to my headteacher the first balaclava which was all my own work. She had been encouraging us to knit them for our forces. This, it seemed to me, was a real war effort.

But even in those dark days we were often able to see the lighter side of life. For instance, one night my brother who was in the Tawstock branch of the Home Guard was on night duty in the village. He was relieved from duty early in the morning to enable him to have time to help with the milking and to take the milk into Barnstaple to the retailer by 8 o'clock. However, by the time he had reached the village all the men who had been with him through the night had gone home and strangers had taken their place. As he was no longer in uniform he was stopped and ordered to show his identity card which he hadn't thought to take with him. He had considerable difficulty in convincing them that he was a 'friend' and not a 'foe'. I reckon that some Barnstaple housewives got their pinta rather late that morning.

In March 1941 change was again my lot. I left school two months before I was due to sit for my 'Higher School Certificate'. Here is the reason: my father had sold his farm. Having been brought up on a stock farm at Arlington he preferred this kind of farming. He now became the tenant of a 200 acre farm called South Radworthy in the Parish of North Molton. His landlord was the Right Honourable Lord Poltimore of Court House, North Molton. He had formerly lived at Court Hall but that was now occupied by an evacuated school from one of our cities. As my brother had promised to stay on as manager of the farm in Tawstock, 'labour' was my father's chief concern. Another problem was how I would travel to and from school each day. So with permission from my headmistress I was allowed to leave school in order to work on the land. This decision, I may add, was at variance with the opinions of some of my other teachers but agriculture was considered to be of prime importance during the war. Education was not even a close second. We were certainly in a favoured position as far as food rationing was concerned. I was surprised recently on turning out my last ration book to see that it was issued for 1953-4.

At times the only help that my father had was that of my sister and myself. What made this so much worse was the high acreage of corn and potatoes that he was compelled to grow. A number of very wet harvesting times made the work even harder. The pitching of the corn sheaves (which had been tied by the binder) to a high corn-rick was straining work. The stony terrain on which we worked played havoc with our wellingtons. Replacements took most of our clothing coupons. Later German prisoners helped us. Some people thought we treated them too well. To us, they were lonely men, a long way from home.

Opportunities for social life was almost non-existent. Our highlight was the North Molton WI's monthly meetings. We walked the three miles as petrol was for essential journeys only. Other war efforts were picking wortleberries (used for dyeing) and collecting foxgloves from which was extracted the drug 'digitalis'.

Despite many difficulties there was much cheerfulness and good humour during these years. No talk of unemployment, burglaries or boredom but a great feeling of togetherness. We were in it together. The National Days of Prayer were well supported.

One night an American plane (Flying Fortress) crashed two miles away on its way back to base after dropping its bombs in Germany. It landed at Sandway, on the Devon and Somerset border. At least eight men were on board. Only two were in a fit condition to seek help. Although they had crashed only 500 yards from a farmhouse, the dense fog and strict blackout precautions prevented its detection. After walking eight miles in three hours they reached a farmhouse at Millbrook at midnight (the home of my future husband). My husband, guided by the men and followed by an ambulance drove to the scene of the accident. Our local policeman also went. On arrival one man was dead, two had broken legs and the others superficial injuries. Several years later two of these men returned asking to be directed back to that spot. On that same moor a searchlight camp was erected. Only once was it in the firing line of the enemy aircraft.

Our North Molton Home Guard was very vigilant. So were the 'Exmoor Mounties'. They hit the headlines. The following extract is from the *Daily Herald* , 2 September 1940 by Dudley Barker.

> *These riders of the moor seem to me almost a perfect example of what the Home Guard should be. I mean of course, in spirit for we cannot all go riding horses across romantic moors. Few of them have ever been soldiers, for farmers must till, not fight. But they have a few old cavalrymen to teach them the essence of the thing.*

Events such as D-Day, Normandy landings, Battle of Britain - familiar events now, but then news was sketchy. It was difficult to sift facts from fiction. Lord Haw Haw's broadcasting propaganda didn't help. Then two new names emerged - Hiroshima and Nagasaki. These places are remembered with mixed feelings!

Anyway we celebrated VE Day. We won - that is if anyone can win a war.

THE YELLOW CONVOY

MR D.W. BRUSH (Plymouth)

During the blitz fire pumps were sent from Bristol but they couldn't be used; wrong connections to hydrants. Many a building could have been saved had all the pumps worked. The fire brigade didn't use the seawater for fear of damaging the pumps, many a building was burnt out on the Barbican.

The Spanish refugees were camped at Marsh Mills. It was said that they lit a bonfire to guide the German planes in, whether it was true never bothered to pursue. Many people of Plymouth left the town and went to places like Cornwood if they thought there was to be a raid, leaving the keys of their houses to neighbours who stopped behind. It was said that they called them the "yellow convoy". Of course the business people moved out altogether, some of them never to return, to places like the Yealm, Bigbury, the moors, anywhere out of it. The static water tanks were installed after all the bombing.

The Indian contingent was stationed around Chaddlewood. Last but not least the lads from southern Ireland, very popular lads, strong, healthy lot - they made many friends. They came here to do bomb damage work. They were good at it, they knew their stuff. But inside work - if there was a right or wrong way to put up a Gyproc 8x4 foot ceiling Paddy knew best. Yes, you guessed, the wrong way!

TANK TESTING AT INSTOW

Dr RONALD COX

There was one memorable period of training which, curiously, I cannot date and which goes unmentioned in the Regimental War Diary and the Regimental History - presumably because we went on it in groups over a period of time rather than all at once. For me that training took place either shortly before we left Bridlington or, much less likely, in the early part of our next posting which was to Aldershot.

It was based on Instow, a small Devon village of indifferent appearance standing midway between the attractive own of Bideford and the equally unattractive town of Barnstaple. Its purposes were tuition in the tactics of waterproofing our tanks and practice in coming ashore from tank landing craft. Clearly the General Staff had D-Day in mind.

The whole process, being secret at the time, is very poorly documented, even at the Imperial War Museum (and, therefore, in subsequent books). But some four months after the Invasion of Normandy, when any ban on publication of the information had been lifted, it was excellently described and illustrated in that splendid magazine, *Picture Post* (October 1944).

The article was entitled 'A Tank Goes for a Swim'. It began:

> *This is the kind of order which we can assume the General Staff addressed to REME (Royal Electrical and Mechanical Engineers) some time ago:*
>
> *You are requested to carry out with utmost speed, thoroughness and secrecy, a project on which the success of future combined operations of a specific nature will depend.*
>
> *Fully to understand your part in the proposed project you will assume the following:*
>
> > *1. A number of tanks of various typed are to be carried on a tank landing craft to a rendezvous 200 yards from a sandy beach held by the enemy. 2. At the point X, where the Tank Landing Craft will stop, the sea is 4'6" (1.37m) deep, with waves riding at 1'6" (46cm). It is high tide. 3. The tanks, under their own motive power, must enter the sea from the ramp of the TLC and wade ashore. 4. On wading ashore the tanks must not only be ready for immediate offensive action, but notwithstanding immersion in the sea, must be capable of carrying on action of an indefinite period.*

We were not in this at the "guinea pig" volunteers stage. When we arrived in the scene the pioneer work had been done and, accordingly to the article quoted above, tanks had already gone ashore in the way described, in the invasion of North Africa. We went to Instow largely to learn all about it.

In essence, the waterproofing had five elements: sealing those parts of the tank which would be under water or which would be damaged by sea spray; ensuring that the expansion gases from the engine could escape; getting the tank safely ashore through, perhaps, six feet (1.8m) of water; making the tank instantly battle-ready when it landed; and ensuring that, if necessary, the tank could operate over a considerable distance while still, largely, in a waterproof state.

The first of these elements involved sealing every joint with black rubbery plastic compounds and/or rubberised fabric. Three photographs in the quoted article show: a plastic compound being fitted round essential mechanical parts, joints in the hull being covered with rubberised fabric and "a secret compound" being used to seal the hatchway in the hull.

The second element required the fitting of a huge canvas or metal exhaust chute on the rear of the tank, adequate in size to cope with the engine gasses, sufficiently high not to take water on board when the tank was in the sea and firmly enough fixed not to be washed away.

The third element involved running the tank down a ramp in the bows of the tank landing craft and ensuring that, by means of the wireless intercom, the driver (who was under water and had initially no vision) was guided ashore safely by the crew commander.

The fourth element, as the *Picture Post* article explained, involved throwing a switch to blow off the cover on the gun and also the exhaust chute. The minor explosion on this account mystified the Germans on D-Day.

Finally, there was substantial road testing to ensure that the vehicle could be driven with the sealant still in place without mechanical breakdown, especially through overheating.

Instow is a west-facing village at the windswept confluence of two rivers, Torridge (on which Bideford stands) and Taw (which flows through Barnstaple). We were billeted in Nissen huts on the sand dunes, between the railway line and the sea. I think the tanks must have been 'resident' ones rather than our own and I have a recollection of only one tank at a time being allowed across the medieval bridge at Bideford because of its inadequacy. The bridge had to be crossed because the starting point for our sea trip was, I think, somewhere near Northam, on the west bank of the Torridge. There we presumably practised driving the tanks on to landing craft (it is astonishing how some of this dramatic action cannot be remembered at all).

I do certainly recollect putting to sea in the tank landing craft, with the tanks on board. I remember, especially, passing the quay at Appledore, watched by a line of silent and doubtless sceptical fishermen. Once we had emerged into Bideford bay we hove to off Northam Burrows, just north of Westward Ho! The ramps of the tank landing craft were then lowered and we ran our tanks down into the water, one by one.

I think we may have done this on two separate occasions, on one of which the water was becoming increasingly choppy, the naval crew and observers being much more sanguine about the weather conditions than we were. My tank went into the water and waded ashore with no difficulty. But one tank (not of my Squadron or, necessarily, of my Regiment) suffered a breakdown of its wireless intercom at the crucial moment. As a result the driver, unable to see (because he was beneath the water) and hearing no instructions, drove in what he thought was a straight line for the shore though in fact the tank had turned and it moved seaward until water started coming into the turret. We didn't have a chance to see whether the driver and co-driver escaped.

There were other hazards, too. On one occasion (I think on the second) we were taken to Northam Burrows on a 3-ton truck which was left standing on the sands. We then went, presumably, to our tanks and carried out the wading exercise. When we returned to the truck we found it bogged down and all our efforts to dislodge it failed. A recovery vehicle was sent for (I assume our tanks had by then been driven away and were uncontactable) but before it arrived the tide came in and we watched, fascinated, as the water gradually crept up the wheels and then into the cabin of the truck. At that point we were collected by another vehicle, so I never saw the end of the saga. The driver, doubtless, had some explaining to do, but he seemed more concerned at the time that he was going to miss a "date" in town (it was a Saturday).

Much more pleasant than the wading exercises, which we carried out in miserable weather, was the subsequent road-testing. For this purpose, we were told to disperse (presumably to avoid too much wear and tear on any one road) and cover x miles by road (not cross-country, but keeping clear of towns) before returning to base. We set off in the general direction of South Molton with a unique sense of freedom; it was a bit like going on a mystery tour instead of being ordered every inch of a pre-arranged way by some higher authority.

We did, however, at one stage run into a difficulty which, though we didn't realise it, was a foretaste of what was to come in Normandy. We went steeply down a very long, winding, narrow country lane with high banks on either side; below us, in the valley, was the magnificent tower of a village church (it might have been West Buckland, but I've never been back that way so I'm not sure). The farther we went, the steeper and more narrow the road became and, finally at a bend we could go no farther without wedging the Sherman. We couldn't turn because of the high banks on either side and so we had to reverse, bit by bit, back the way we had come. It gave Corporal McCafferty, my crew commander, excellent training in precise driver instruction, it gave the driver (who might have been Pete Reagan) good experience in reacting swiftly and accurately to orders he was given, and it certainly put the waterproofing to the test. The engine didn't overheat, but the amount of petrol consumed must have been horrendous. Fortunately during the whole of the hour or so spent in that length of Devon county lane we met no vehicle wanting to pass in either direction, something unimaginable in the 1990s!

EYEWITNESS TO THE BLITZ

MRS E. CURTIS (Exeter)

I was thirteen years old when it was announced over my Grandmother's radio that England was at war with Germany. There was a lot of hustle and bustle making blackout curtains which was a little scary but life seemed to go on much the same for some while. I joined Boots the Chemist at sixteen years as an assistant. In those days you were given a good training especially on the drug counter, there was no National Health and people who could not afford to go to the Doctor, came to us for advice on their health problems so we had to know what we were doing. I spent the first year helping in the dispensary getting to know the drugs, filling up the half empty drug containers, with the dispenser keeping his beady eye on me, compressing the powder he had dispensed into tablet form. Very few goods were pre-packed, glouber salts, Epsom salts, magnesium powders etc. were all kept in the little drawers labelled in Latin at the back of the counter, having first been weighed in the drug stock room into two- and four-ounce packets.

We all took it in turns to fire-watch on the firms' premises for incendiary bombs, four of us at a time. We slept in the upstairs library on camp beds. Boots at that time was on the corner of Queen Street where C & A now stands. A restaurant under C & A was our stock rooms. Everyone was doing their bit for the war effort and I joined the Women's Voluntary Service and spent two or three nights a week after work washing dishes until quite late after the evening meal at the Royal Devon and Exeter Hospital. No dishwashers in those days. Everyone over eighteen was in the forces so it was the very young and old who did this work. The Exeter Museum was the venue for the Allied Forces Canteen and here after work I also helped with cutting up sandwiches and making tea and coffee for the forces. At home we were provided with a Morrison Shelter, an iron table which could be removed during the day for eating and put back when there was a raid. My father had spinal problems and wasn't called up. He became a Fire Warden with others in the road too old and not fit enough for service.

The Blitz... Exeter had several attacks by air and although we heard Lord Haw Haw, the German propagandist, over the radio say "the streets of Exeter, 'the Golden City of the West' would run with blood", we doubted it would. How wrong we were! The sirens sounded that awful night in May but my sisters and I decided not to get up. My mother had got my younger brothers from their beds and kept calling for us to come down, and then the first bomb came down. It sounded so close we fell out of bed, down the stairs and into the Morrison Shelter, not before the second bomb came down. It was the most terrifying experience.

The bombs whistled down one after another. We were all crammed in, eight of us including my mother. Father was outside doing his duty and stayed there until it was all over, two and half hours of hell. My mother was screaming for him to come in and my youngest brother seemed to do a somersault with every bomb, putting his little head down and covering his ears with his hands. As the eldest I tried to protect him, my mother did her best with my youngest sister who was about five years old. We clung to each other as the planes roared above us dropping their evil weapons. Suddenly there was an almighty explosion, much worse than the others. I think we all died for a moment. Everyone was deathly quiet and we thought the end was near, but no, the bombs continued until at last the planes died away. Still we sat in that little cramped container too frightened to move when my father came in and told us it seemed to be all over. We crawled out one by one too dazed and frightened for words. Then we looked out of the window and someone screamed "Our school is on fire!" The sky was bright red but it turned out later, it wasn't the school, but the almost complete destruction of the city. Our front door had been blown off its hinges and the bedroom ceilings had fallen down on our beds, but apart from that it was the only damage to our house.

The next day my father and I tried to get to work, not knowing the full extent of the damage. We lived overlooking the higher cemetery so we walked up Pinhoe Road and there, halfway up, were the results of the very loud explosion, several houses, six I believe, had been demolished by a land mine. The ambulances were there and the dead bodies were being brought out. To a sixteen year old it was nauseating. In those days in the early forties, we knew little about death, not having televisions. We continued to the top of Sidwell Street, many roads were cordoned off with 'unexploded bomb' notices, and there before out eyes was the 'Golden City' completely in ruins. We could see as far as the Cathedral and there, it stood out in all its glory amidst the rubble of Exeter, proud and defiant, a comfort to us all - a sight I shall never forget. I looked at my father as he stood there quietly weeping and then we both wept. We made our way home but not before noticing a body, covered with a sheet awaiting collection on the pavement. Where once rows and rows of little houses stood called Newtown they now lay flattened to the ground.

Later that day a loudspeaker told us we could go to Broadclyst where the village hall would be open that night if we didn't want to stay in Exeter in case of another raid. We took pillows and blankets and were looked after by two young NCO Royal Air Force cadets, pupils of Hele's School. Being the same age, my friend and I sat up most of the night talking to them.

The next day my father took my mother and the younger children to Yeovil hoping that they would be safer there. I refused to leave my father alone, and so I was alone that afternoon when there was a knock on the door and one of the young NCOs stood there. He told me his uncle was missing who had been working in Exeter. He had rung the hospitals and police who told him to try the mortuary. His aunt was an invalid, as was his father, would I go with him? I said I would if my friend of the night before would come with us. We arrived at the mortuary gate, but the two of us were too nervous to go in and waited outside. He was gone for a very long time and eventually we went in search of him, we faced a corridor with doors with windows blown out and there we glimpsed dead bodies, we turned on our heels and fled. My friend didn't eat for five days. The young seventeen year old NCO was apparently asked to clean up the bodies with other Senior Hele's School boys.

Days later, we witnessed a mass burial in the corner of the cemetery, from our netted bedroom windows. I believe the Last Post was played but my memory isn't so good these days. There were German pilots also buried nearby.

Now as I sit and paint in my garden, high on the Blackdown Hills, and study the beautiful cloud formations, looking down this lovely Otter Valley to Exeter, it is hard to remember these lovely skies were once the venue for many, many German planes that rained down bombs on the innocent people of Exeter.

SALUTE THE LUMBER JILL!

MRS MAVIS DANKS

Although not born a Devonian, Devon became my adoptive county when my parents moved to Newton Abbot in late 1941, for during the Blitz - the heavy sustained bombing of Liverpool - our home was virtually destroyed, as was Father's tailoring business. Unable to afford insurance during the Depression years of the 1930s he was forced to abandon his home to become the manager of a tailoring business in the market town of Newton Abbot. Mind you it was not a bad swap from derelict, war-torn Liverpool to the relative peace and beauty of Devon, was it? Early in 1942 I decided that it was time that I made up my mind what role I could play in the war effort before I was conscripted. I opted for the Land Army, although I must admit that farm animals especially cows held no fascination for me. However at the interview I was given the option of joining a "new force" which was being formed, designated the Women's Timber Corps. This was to be a mobile force which would replace the lumberjacks working in our forests. Due to enlistment their numbers were fast dwindling. Wood could no longer be imported from abroad as German U-boats were playing havoc with our shipping so cargo space was at a premium. Wood was a necessity for so many purposes.

The Women's Timber Corps you ask yourself. Never heard of it! Oh, come on, surely some of you Devonians must have seen us in our green berets, crossed axes on our sleeves, flashes on our shoulders sporting our brown fir tree badge, for many of us worked at some time in your County. Let me tell you a little about it. In March 1942 the first 120 recruits assembled at a station in Suffolk, to be herded into Army lorries bumped and shaken to a camp at Culford to be housed in ten huts of twenty.

P.E. at 6.30am every morning found muscles that we never knew we had. Life was somewhat spartan, but we were usually too tired to complain. We were young, willing (in most cases) and able (in fewer cases). We were divided into four groups, spending a week of training in each.

Forestry in all its aspects was to be our business. Supervised by an experienced forester we were taught how to swing an axe, how to make a V-shape in the bole of the tree having decided in which direction it was to fall, and if necessary using a cross-cut saw. We then lopped (removed the branches) with axe or bill-hook, topped and sawed it up into pit-props according to size. The brushwood had to be burned so knowledge of making a "safe" fire was necessary, and anyway we had to boil our water in billies if we wanted a cup of : "char". Then to the saw-mills. Initially this was quite frightening amongst whizzing machinery, often without safety guards but planks of different sizes did emerge perhaps for railway sleepers, for building or utility furniture.

Haulage was the third discipline. Tractors or lorries were used but there were few who could drive. We were taught how to attach the winch rope from a tractor to a tree to get it to the sawing ramp; we were taught how to carry large props on our shoulders; how to load a lorry safely and how to stack. At this I was not a success. I was too small! Although I could carry a prop to a lorry the loaders found that they had difficulty in bending down far enough to take it from me!

The last section was measuring; the office and paperwork, so for this there had to be some mathematical bent. Yards, metres, chains, girth, piece-work rates, pay packets and later P.A.Y.E. Having worked as a book-keeper for the three years prior to joining I opted for forestry!

We were posted in groups to all parts of the country, six of us being posted to a remote village in Shropshire to board with the village headmistress. Most of the work here was clearing and burning ready for replanting. From here I went with Rita to a village near Welshpool where pit-props were produced mainly. Promoted to a ganger I was sent to Hereford and then on to Cornwall as a sub-forewoman. Here both Timber Corps and civilians including gypsies and their horses worked side by side. It was a huge operation where all the trees were felled and converted into pit-props, which were stacked awaiting loading into railway trucks for despatch to the mines. Brushwood was burned and the undergrowth was cleared. Perhaps our most important job was the making of charcoal, a very skilled art. Fortunately this was supervised by an experienced local man. After almost two years the forest was bare, and so I was posted to a village on the edge of Dartmoor and Devon.

By this time larger groups of girls were being housed in hostels but I had always been in local billets, some of which were very good and some extremely poor. It was the luck of the draw. Few had running water or inside toilet facilities. Usually water was obtained from an outside iron hand-pump or water butt, while toilets were of the "bucket and chuck-et" type a hole in a plank placed over a bucket or a ditch.

We had all learned to accept and make the best of wherever we were placed, but naturally we were always apprehensive about "the next one". In this case I need not have worried. I caught a bus from one of the larger towns, kit-bag slung over one shoulder, my case in the other hand, heading towards South Molton. The bus driver obligingly stopped outside a whitewashed house, the walls covered in a tumble of climbing roses, the garden glowing with colour from the masses of multicoloured flowers. The farmer and some of his workers stood at the end of the garden awaiting my arrival, perhaps expecting an Amazon, doffing their caps at my approach. The tallest of the men came forward hand outstretched.

"Welcome! Welcome Maid", he said in a rich Devon accent. A plump rosy-cheeked motherly woman stood at the door arms outstretched to hug me as I reached her, escorted by my male guard of honour. I felt like royalty!

Immediately I was seated at a larger kitchen table laden with food including scones, jam and lashings of cream aware that four pairs of eyes were watching my every move. Soon two tall handsome young men entered to be introduced as her sons, Charlie and Gordon.

My bedroom was large with gaily flowered curtains at the window looking over the fields at the back, and there was even a vase of flowers on the dressing table. Next morning I was awakened with a cup of tea, and a jug of steaming hot water was placed on the marble-topped wash stand. Hot water! Sheer Luxury! Charlie offered to take me to the site on the back of his motor cycle. Hair raising! The Foreman introduced me to several gangs of girls who were mostly preparing felled trees, lopping, topping and stripping, for telegraph poles and bagging pulpwood, but their welfare was to be my main concern.

On VE Day the lorry took us into Barnstaple on two days leave. We were lucky to find accommodation in a hostel run by a religious order I think. Lights were on everywhere, doors wide open, anything that could be banged was banged. People sang, people danced and we were drawn into the festivities unstintingly. Two very happy days!

I unfortunately had begun to turn yellow, jaundice being diagnosed. My dear landlady kindly offered to look after me but I opted to go home to Newton Abbot, after fond farewells. I would have liked to have told you more of the Lumber Jills the women who ensured that the mines had the pit-props to produce the fuel for the factories which produced munitions; for the bakers' ovens, for the trains, for the telegraph poles to maintain communications; the railway sleepers, the charcoal for explosives etc, wood for repairs, building and furniture. In fact, for at least four years, if anything was made of wood or from wood it was probably produced by a Lumber Jill. Salute the Lumber Jill! NOTE: Mrs Danks has published her reminiscences in a book *Lumber Jill* (Ex Libris Press, 1994).

INFERNO IN DEVONPORT

MRS J. DUBICKI-MATTHEWS

If I had taken heed of a warning from a stranger in a doorway that night I would not be alive to day to tell this tale. I lived beside Devonport Dockyard and on the night in question I was revisiting the hotel where I worked as a bar girl. It was my evening off. I had promised the girls who worked with me, that I would meet them in the lounge. The place quickly filled with naval personnel. They were a jolly lot, as in the war years everyone seemed drawn to one another in a spirit of camaraderie which is sadly lacking today.

My parents kept a small public house further down the hill beside the dockyard wall but I was helping out here in the hotel, the former bar girl having recently married, until a replacement could be found. It was very busy now "Johno" and "Bugsy Baker", two of our customers, were jesting with us and telling us to get behind the counter and serve them, when a sudden hush came over the lounge as the voice of Lord Haw Haw spoke over the radio from Germany, telling us that Devonport would be bombed at nine o' clock that same night.

It was now nearly nine, we looked at one another not knowing what to think when suddenly the world outside seemed to go haywire. The place shook as deafening thuds sounded outside, then the doors opened and several wardens appeared, telling everyone to go down to the cellar below as the whole place outside was alight with thousands of incendiary bombs and soon the explosive bombs would follow in their wake. The door opened again, I could see a red glow in the sky. Voices were crying out from the burning buildings opposite, then we were all bundled down into the cellar. I knew I had to get out and go home as quickly as I could; my mother would be frantic knowing I was out. I was afraid she would not go into the small stone shelter (which was built on to an outside wall of the house) without me.

I made an excuse of wanting to go to the toilet, running into the courtyard. I found the tall back door was locked and bolted, a high stone wall sheltered the hotel from the street outside. I don't know how I climbed over the wall but within seconds I was standing in the street in the middle of "Dante's Inferno".

It is hard to believe now that the holocaust I saw before me was happening in a civilised world. To my right was a high hill above the dockyard wall, which I had to run down before turning off at the bottom. The road on the hill was strewn with thousands of incendiary bombs standing on end like huge glowing candles, on my left houses were burning each side of a narrow street, red hot debris was flying everywhere, cries of "help!" were all around me, above in the red glowing sky, the German Luftwaffe looked like locusts, the heavy drone of their engines denoted that they were weighted with bombs. I crossed over on to the hill. I was so high up now, it seemed as if I too was up there with the enemy. In the glow of searchlights I saw bombs dropping like pellets, then came explosions each side of me, the target being the dockyard to which I was running parallel alongside. The road ahead was lit like a runway. Going back hours later after the all-clear I found the hill was filled with bomb craters, so I was glad I had left early when the lighted hill was probably being used as a guide.

I was running now in and out of the "candles" staring ahead, my brain frozen with fear, my coat flying out behind me I was saying over and over, "God help me! God help me!" I came to the lower road now, running in the middle as if in a nightmare, my lungs were bursting, each side of me houses were burning, cries came over the smoke filled breeze, my coat was discarded as it was burning also. Suddenly, as I neared the corner on my left, I beheld what seemed to be a sheet coming down towards me. Someone in the doorway on my right shouted "get in here quick, you'll be killed", I turned my head slightly and saw a young sailor in the doorway but I kept on running I had only gone a couple of yards when instinct made me drop to the ground, I felt the hard pavement as I crossed my arms over my head, that action saved my life, when the land mine dropped only a few feet away.

All hell was let loose. Bricks, buildings, everything seemed to go sky high. I will never forget the noise as the debris flew around me, or the blast from the mine that swept past me like a whirlwind of pressure that drew every breath out of my body.

Just reaching that corner and almost turning it had prevented me from being in a direct line of the blast. When I got up and turned, like Lot's wife, I wish I hadn't for the huge corner block where the young sailor had called to me had disappeared.

At my feet were remnants of a body. I turned and ran. Someone from a nearby shelter tried to drag me in but I scratched like a wild thing and they let me go again. I reached our shelter and ran in. My mother was there with my father and customers from our little pub. They were sitting packed like sardines, drinking from huge jugs; you'd have thought they were on a picnic. Someone shouted "Nell, your pub's been hit!" as another wave came and took our breaths away. I scrambled on our roof with a hosepipe and tried to put out the blaze.

Later, when the all clear sounded, a friend and I walked back along the route I had taken earlier. Rubble and debris were everywhere. Large craters where the bombs had fallen made our journey difficult. The lounge of the hotel where I had worked was completely demolished. Wardens and nurses were carrying injured into the hospital nearby.

On returning I remarked to my parents that I would sleep in the small stone shelter which would be more peaceful to my mind than the shattered public house which was still smouldering.

I awoke in the morning to find an air raid warden shaking me, telling me to hurry and get out, as the shelter was cordoned off with rope. A huge unexploded bomb (one of the largest) had fallen through the roof of the house to which the shelter was attached and was lying under the floor of the shelter, ticking away. I remarked that I had stayed there to sleep as it had seemed more peaceful, especially listening to the tick of what I thought was a grandfather clock coming from a room in the house. I went outside to see my parents. We were all told to move away as an unexploded bomb lay in the entrance to our public house, called Smokey Joe's.

We stood, not knowing what to do or where to go, when a voice behind us said "Would anyone like to come into my house and have a boiled egg?" It was Beat Tricks, our helper, and we all sat in her kitchen, a boiled egg in our hands, amongst the rubble. It was the best meal I have ever tasted. I silently thanked God for bringing us through that terrible night.

GLIDER PILOT

PETER FLETCHER (Plymouth)

The very first troops into France on D-Day were not the seaborne troops nor the paratroops but Horsa gliders, flown by men of the Glider Pilot Regiment. Six gliders, each carrying twenty men, landed almost on the bridges over the River Orne and the Canal. These bridges were captured intact before they could be blown up.

Next a brigade of paratroops landed with one of its duties to try and clear some of the "anti-invasion posts, gliders for the destruction of" which had suddenly appeared a week before D-Day.

I was the pilot of one of the 67 gliders which landed - or attempted to land - in the dark at 3.00 am some seven miles in from the beaches, carrying a maximum load of a jeep and trailer plus five men.

This followed months and months of training, making bigger and bigger massed landings, then training with the 6th Airborne Division. As we had been reminded so often, pilots we were, but soldiers first; flying a glider was just a more interesting way of going to battle. Having joined this strange regiment as a private I was now a Lieutenant, and was blessed with an unflappable Scot, Sgt Shiells, as my second pilot.

The build-up to D-Day was impressive as we were given information about the gigantic size of the whole operation. Near Caen, we were told - where on earth was it, and how the hell do you pronounce Caen? An anxious rush to the maps. Later a sand map was made, a camera run over the intended flight path and the film was shown to us in half light to give us an idea how it would look at 3.00 a.m. from 2,000 feet.

Crews were chosen, special jobs allocated. Our tugs were Albermarles, only twin engined and not really man enough for the job, and with a loaded glider they needed every inch of the 2,000 yard runway at Harwell. We had a "last supper" in the mess at 10 o'clock, for some I'm afraid it was just that. Then to the runway where half the station had come to see us off, 67 gliders and tugs made an impressive sight.

Every time I see the film of Henry V with the camp scenes before the battle, I am reminded of that hour before take-off - groups of people strolling around, joking with our friends not chosen for this operation, checking weapons, wanting to get on with it, wanting above all to get a good lift-off. As with any flying, in the air is no bother, it's getting up and down that causes the problems. Without engines we had to judge our landing first time every time!

Then the order to get on board. I checked again that the jeep and trailer were securely lashed. I had a chat with the Major and his men and went over the ditching drill. The pilot is in charge whatever the rank of the "live load". The Major seemed a little stuffy, probably just nervous. I said that, as far as I was concerned, they could smoke, but to be doubly careful. They were surrounded by highly inflammable wood plus petrol in the jeep - and none of us carried parachutes!

Our tug pulled in front of us, the tow rope was attached, strain taken and we were racing down the runway. I eased the wheel back and we had lift-off before the tug, so I kept just above him as he came "unstuck" and we were safely up. Sgt Shiells had his hand on the tail trim control and at a nod from me eased it forward as we seemed a bit tail heavy. We then settled down for the two-hour flight, taking it in turn to hold our position slightly above the Albermarle to be clear of his slipstream. Just as being towed in a car needs concentration, so it does in the air, with the added dimension of up and down movement. The tow rope must be kept taut, a slack rope followed by the inevitable jerk can make it break.

The exhileration began to wear off and I wondered whether this operation was perhaps just a little too hazardous. You glide in at nearly 100 m.p.h in the dark, a lot of gliders would be heading for the same area, and we had no idea whether the paras had been able to clear any of the anti-invasion posts. Mass landings in daylight are spectacular but not difficult, and we had never tried more than just a few landings together at night for the rather sinister reason that we could not afford to lose many gliders.

Too late to start worrying now we were approaching the coast. Patches of cloud, flack slowly reaching up for us, one burst between tug and glider. We were through and clear, the black ground beneath us. I handed over to Shiells. Forward and to our right the white ribbons of the parallel river and canal. I called up our tug skipper and thanked him for the trip, wished him safe returns, and said we would pull off soon. A quiet look round, a few deep breaths as I judged the distance to glide. The church of Ranville ahead so I pulled off. The sudden quiet as we slowed to 100 m.p.h. Another glider passed us, going too fast.

Started our 180 degree turn over the church tower, a little too high, so put on half flap. Levelled up for the run in, going too fast so full flap when touching down with posts all around us. Brakes hard on, mowed posts down, then a small bank not visible in the aerial photographs. The nose wheel up into our cabin and demolished it. Sgt Shiells in a heap over his broken control column but unhurt, so he said - not true, some ribs damaged.

Our load intact. We climbed out, mightily relieved, and started to unload the jeep as gliders with horrendous noise crash-landed around us. Of the 67 due on that landing zone all but twelve succeeded - a figure infinitely better than expected.

Another 300 gliders landed on the afternoon of D-Day. The seaborne troops reached us by midday, headed by the sound of bagpipes and Brigadier Lord Lovat and his commandos - and very welcome they were!

TEENAGER IN THE BLITZ

MRS BARBARA HALLS

I was fourteen when the Second World War broke out. For the last two years I had been conscious that my parents were very worried that there might be another war. I was playing with my brother in the woods where the telephone exchange now stands, near Crownhill, on that sunny September morning, when a friend came to tell us that war had been declared. The announcement had seemed inevitable for some time and didn't mean a lot to us children but we could see how worried our parents were.

The next day there was a trial sounding of the air raid warning and all clear sirens. When I heard the first one I was extremely scared but I realised that from now on there would be many more and it was no use feeling frightened. When the real raids came I did not have that terrified feeling again; I think it was the prospect of another night's loss of sleep that bothered me most. There were disappointments too; at school our half-term holidays were cancelled, and the school leavers' party, "in view of the national emergency."

I left school at sixteen and became a very junior member of the staff of Plymouth City Library. I remember going to work in the black-out and, because we were on double summer time for the duration in the winter, it meant getting up on raw, cold mornings. When I could, I cycled. There were often traffic hold-ups where roads had been bombed overnight and I would find myself stuck behind an open truck covered with signs saying "Danger, unexploded bomb" and grinning soldiers sitting in the back beside the bomb. Sometimes roads were closed off with tapes but we all just popped underneath rather than making a detour.

The most frightening time was when I was on the late shift one evening. The siren went and all borrowers and staff went down to the basement to wait for the "all clear". Some of the seniors made tea and took it to the public in one part of the basement. We juniors were in a part where there was a table-tennis table and we took it in turns to play. As the air-raid became more intense the noise of the bombs falling was funnelled down the well of the large service lift. The sound of the bombs screaming down in that enclosed space was truly terrifying. Afterwards my friend and I walked home, picking our way over hoses while fire-fighters tried to quell the flames as Sherwell Church burned.

One day I cycled to work and found that the road behind the museum and library had a tape across it so I dodged underneath to find that the whole library was a burnt-out shell. The caretakers were rescuing what they could from the basement and we carried saturated leather-bound volumes of *The Times* up the road, where they were spread on the pavement to dry in the warm sun. They were so heavy it took two girls to carry each volume. This seemed to go on for days, though I don't suppose it did; the smell of burnt paper makes me feel sick even now. After this we were deployed to help the city services in issuing travel vouchers to people who were bombed out.

Later, an art gallery in the museum was allocated to the library and all books that were returned or donated were catalogued and classified ready to re-open in the Plymouth Room. Lord Astor performed the opening ceremony on about 28 July 1941. We were able to expand and move downstairs to a larger room after a few months.

Branch duties were interesting too. Every time it was my turn to go to St Budeaux there had been a bomb blast nearby the night before and my colleague and I had to clear up the mess, put back the books and get the issues in order. There was no way of knowing when the books were due back. We were always lucky to get books back, anyway.

The Laira Branch Library was situated in a cell of the old Police Station and owing to shortage of staff, the caretaker, Mrs Westlake, kept the library running very well. One of the staff did duty there once a week. The most moving experience I had was late one afternoon when I was in Crownhill Branch Library. It was very quiet that day, with few borrowers. I became aware of a strange noise which went on and on. I looked out of the window and saw that the road was filled with people; they were pushing carts, barrows, prams and were laden with bags. Some of the prams had children piled in and some were piled high with bags and blankets. There was no sound of voices, just the sound of feet as the people wearily, steadily walked up to the moor to get some kind of sleep safely away from the bombs. It was a sight I shall never forget. The wonderful thing was that everyone came back next morning to carry on as well as they could through the latest devastations. The spirit of Plymouth was truly great.

NORMANDY DIARY

MR BERT HITCHEN (Cullompton)

I joined an infantry regiment in 1942 which had just changed to light anti-aircraft and spent a few weeks on Salisbury Plain forming up as a division to go out to the Western Desert, but later the division was split so we spent two years along the south and east coasts with our 40mm Bofors guns. We did a lot of practice firing and quite often the real thing as well. We practised landing from craft with ramps and one all-day exercise out in the English Channel with lots of air cover.

In early 1944 the Bofors were taken off their chassis and three barrelled 20mm Oerlikons fitted in their places with equal numbers on Crusader tanks. The Oerlikons were electrically controlled by one man with a joystick for elevation and traverse with three buttons on the stick enabling the operator to fire any or all guns while sitting in an armour-plated cockpit - much safer than the loaders.

Two weeks before we sailed we were in a sealed camp with some of the 1st Canadian Army who were later seen on the other side, as our main job was the defence of vital roads and bridges.

At last we moved to Felixstowe and boarded landing crafts with all our gear for a grand adventure but became somewhat disheartened when the landings were delayed for 24 hours and our officer told us 80 per cent casualties were expected. However we could not jump off, being somewhere in the English Channel heading for "the far side" as General Eisenhower called Normandy.

On looking around we saw we were joining the armada, which was a reassuring sight and gave us added courage for later. When we sailed in to the beaches and lowered the ramp one gun was towed behind each tank towards a distant gap in the sea wall with us staggering behind with wet feet and legs for a hundred yards or so. We passed damaged tanks and other vehicles with a number of assault troops in the sand. Sporadic shelling was in progress from the enemy but I did not notice any small arms fire, although we got off the beach as fast as possible to a sandy track which had tapes on each side, meaning that mines had been lifted or detonated by the engineers who had flail tanks to help them. The track took us through the sand dunes to a permanent road into the village of Ver-sur-Mer where we had a welcome from a villager with a two-gallon jar of wine, but we refrained from drinking as we had been warned about poison in water and had our water in special jerrycans all the way from England.

After looking at a sketch map supplied on our way up the road by one of our officers with a bike, who must have landed with an earlier wave, we moved off the main road at the far end of the village into a large field behind a farmhouse where the cows were chained up. This was handy for the milk as some of us country lads could do the milking by kneeling on one knee and filling a dixie one-handed. We unhitched the gun in a suitable corner of the field and the tank which towed us moved up to the battle area a few miles on, leaving us to level up and get ready for action when required, as the village had one main street with houses either side and was one of the few good roads to Cepon and beyond, used by every type of vehicle and by marching troops heading for battle.

Sarge said, "Dig yourselves a slit trench", so Den and I dug a long one for the two of us, as we had often slept nose to tail on cold nights when out in the open in England, but now it was quite warm, so at two feet deep we gave up digging as we were tired out after bouncing about on the trip over, which had made us feel dead on our feet.

Later the gun roster was sorted out for the night between nine of us with one NCO and two gunners on each shift, two hours on and four off - one man for firing and two loaders. I was on duty from two to four, so off came my shoes in the early evening for the first time for days - how many I never knew as we lost track of days. At dusk planes came over to attack the beaches so all hell was let loose from all directions, especially from the Navy, who would shoot at anything with wings, so no sleep that night.

At first light, about 5 a.m. we opened a ration pack containing tinned and dried foods, tea and cigs (no danger of lung cancer as we had 50 cigs to divide among the nine of us) so after a smoke I said "What do you fancy for breakfast?" After looking at the hard biscuits, which you could eat for hours and still not be satisfied, I decided to go down to the village to supplement the rations. Knocking on a door a few yards down the street I was greeted by a man who said "Come in, Tommy. What can I get for you?" I tried my French: "Dooze erf e' du pane s'il vou plait." He said "Wait a few minutes and my daughter will be down to get the things you want, but in the meantime have a drop of Calvados." This he poured from a bottle into two glasses and he downed his in one go and so, forgetting the poison warnings, I drank mine in one gulp, which took my breath away and left me gasping - a casualty, perhaps? I looked at my watch and he said "What's the hurry? It's only six o'clock." Then his daughter came in and he used my French for the eggs and bread, which gave us a good laugh - and more Calvados. Eventually I left the house and staggered back to the gun. The sarge said that it had taken some time but he has happy when we got a nice breakfast cooked on our petrol fuelled camping type stove with fresh milk in the tea, which had been procured by one of the boys. He had been reprimanded in French but of course he replied suitably in army English!

We stripped the gun and tested it as per the book, ready for more action, but a message was received stopping all firing for 24 hours as the fighters on our side had been caused more damage than the Luftwaffe the previous day and night. So I looked around the area from the field which had a four foot high stone wall, in some places worse for wear. On the north side was a lane to numerous small fields and on the west was a field of potatoes, but *Achtung Minen* signs were all around the edges. On the south side was an orchard. The enemy were a few miles away but at night Shermans were laagered there, but their numbers decreased nightly and eventually only badly damaged ones remained. To the east was the farm and village which we defended.

A searchlight arrived later and was set up in the opposite corner of the field, which pleased us as from experience we knew that planes came down the line of the light with all guns blazing which actually happened a few nights later but only the light went out with no-one injured. Some nights later a sniper was firing at us from beside the haystack in the far corner of the potato field, so I took the Bren gun, placed it in the wall as near as possible to the rifleman, waited for a flash, then fired a few rounds on auto and the firing stopped. Next day I went up the lane to where the firing had come from but all I found were a few empty cases from an ordinary rifle. What a marksman!

Something good - I noticed that someone had been digging potatoes so later we decided that the warning signs for mines had been put there by the owners of the field as protection. What a hope with the British army around! Anyway new potatoes were on the menu from then on.

The RASC arrived a few days later and unloaded all sorts of stores on the south side of the field, so it was goodbye to our slit trenches which we did not use as shelling from the enemy had petered out, although the swish from the shells passing over from our warships was scary at times. We often wondered how the shells in flight missed the fighter planes which used a temporary landing strip a couple of miles up the road to rearm and refuel all day.

Some days later we moved to the Caen Canal about a mile from Ouistreham to defend a temporary bridge which was being shot up by German fighter planes in daylight, so that at night soldiers from a bridge company had to replace the damaged supports - a noisy job ("Heave ho! Heave ho!") on this vital bridge used by a lot of our forces fighting to the east.

Later our THQ arrived and camped in the quarry on the west side of the Canal and, as we were over the bridge on the danger side, I walked down to Ouistreham and borrowed a rowing boat which we kept handy on our side for fishing and crossing the Canal in an emergency. I managed a trip to Ver-sur-Mer with a few damaged German helmets, called at my egg man, and we went down to the beaches and exchanged our goods for cigs and chocolates with the sailors who gave generously for souvenirs. On the way back we called in for a drop of Calvados and I was given a new pipe and some home-grown tobacco which nearly choked me for a while, but I persevered and, by the time the NAAFI van came around, I was a true pipe smoker and started on St Bruno, which I continued with until 1982 when I finished smoking altogether.

At that time we suffered with the "Normandy glide", which was probably caused by the flies which were numerous and got everywhere, although I made a safe for our food with a ventilated door. They used to sit all over it and, when the door was opened, in they went, so it was difficult keep our food free from infection. I was affected with the glide for two weeks and also eaten at night by mosquitos, which could sent their nozzle through blankets and were interested in biting you around the eyes. We had to completely cover ourselves when sleeping with a gas cape and groundsheet - no polythene sheeting then.

We were dug in the side of the canal where the bank was about 6 feet above water level and on the other side was a stone-surfaced road wide enough for vehicles to travel on but, being under observation from the German battery at Sallenelles, it was not used by many as shelling and sniping was a danger and it was signed appropriately. Later a company of infantry camped in the wood by us while they attacked the gun site, which was a difficult job as marshes between the canal and the River Orne made it impossible for a tank attack and the only road was mined and covered in concrete boxes. Eventually after losing quite a few men the position was captured from the defenders who were a cycle troop. Most were killed and a few taken prisoner, leaving us a few bikes as souvenirs which we took with us to a new site about 200 yards north of Pegasus Bridge at Benouville. This was a great place to be as a cafe was open most of the day and night so liquid lunches were normal when funds allowed and no duty. ME109s led by a FW190 came over shooting all around with cannons and an odd rocket but we had no casualties at this site, although a daylight raid by hundreds of our low-flying bombers made us get our heads down. Caen was their objective but, like all bomb aimers, they sometimes missed the target.

Our next move was nearer to Beauville in a field where we had a fairly peaceful time with our first cookhouse and kitchen built by a few of us. It was timber framed and had corrugated walls and its roof was covered with our camouflage net. HQ brought us a bell tent to sleep in so we recruited some villagers to do the chores with payment in kind: food, chocolates and cigs. The enemy had left Caen and were getting plastered at Falaise which we visited to collect two van-type vehicles which the officers had converted, one to a bathroom with water tank on the roof and a heater and shower inside, the other like a NAAFI van with a drop-down side as a control room with wireless, maps etc. Somewhere around this time some ships used the canal again as fighting had ceased in the area so we said goodbye to our friends and helpers leaving all our unofficial goods to them as we drove on to Pont l'Eveque, our next site.

Compiled from my 1944 diary.

PRELUDE TO D DAY

MR J. HOLWELL (aged nine in 1944)

I vividly remember visiting an aunt who lived on what is now Normandy Way Hill. Such visits were a weekly event but suddenly towards the end of May my mother had to apply - to whom I do not know - for a permit to visit my aunt. On 5 June we paid her a visit, but from about midway up Pemros Road we were escorted by U.S. Army police to the aunt's house and given a specific time to be ready to go home. If we failed to be ready at the given time we would have to stay the night!

From the front of my aunt's house the river was "choc a block" with ships, some fully laden and others being loaded with men and equipment from the Vicarage Road Camp. It appeared to me that it would be possible to walk from Saltash Passage across to Saltash from one ship's deck to another. My mother and I returned home after the visit and I remember the radio announcement on D-Day informing the nation that allied forces has landed on the beaches of northern France.

On a subsequent visit to my aunt she told me that, after going to bed having seen the mass of assembled ships, the next morning the river was completely empty. She often wondered how many of the embarked troops survived the landings.

In the build-up to D-Day I often visited another aunt who lived in Ivybridge. On a visit to her I met my first black person. Apparently the camp situated up the road from my aunt's house was occupied predominantly by black troops who had caused some public order problems in the town. On the occasion of my visit the commanding officer and a senior black soldier were paying a visit to apologise for the damage caused to her property. The compensation offered included my first taste of a Hershey bar.

Another highlight was a party held at Seaton Barracks at which I and my classmates experienced ice-cream, pancakes, white bread and "candies" hitherto unobtainable due to rationing.

AMERICANS IN TORQUAY

MISS A.G. ILLINGWORTH

Duiring the war I was for over four years in the A.T.S, serving as a transport driver firstly for the War Office taking despatches from the War Office in Cheltenham to the War Office in London. I was then posted to a R.A.S.C. OCTU in Southend for twelve months. Around the middle of 1943 I was given a compassionate posting to Tavistock and eventually to my home in Torquay where I remained until I was demobbed at the end of the war. After a short while driving for a unit based at the Prudential huts in Shiphay Lane I was then moved to join the staff of Colonel Williams the Quartering Commandant for South Devon. Our HQ was at Danvers in Wheatridge Lane. The staff consisted of the Colonel, three Captains a Sergeant and several Civilian Clerks.

For the first six months our time was occupied in requisitioning suitable properties in readiness for the arrival of the American troops in preparation for D-Day. This was a most interesting assignment as we were responsible for the whole of South Devon, not only as driver - I was also responsible for the inventories of the various properties surveyed for occupation. Each week we covered a wide area relying very much on map references as the signposts had been taken down but not removed, so as long as we knew where we had come from, we were not lost for very long.

We made many visits to the properties when occupied by the Americans and made many good friends as they were so hospitable. It was my job to escort the Americans to their billets in Torquay, when they arrived at Torquay Station, or "Torqway" as they called it.

I well remember the American troops sitting on the footpath in Victoria Parade awaiting embarkation on D-Day, a long wait, as D-Day was delayed 24 hours.

So many I recognised, many who would not return, especially our own Sergeant Edyvean who was killed on landing in France.

On D-Day I was standing on Berry Head with the Colonel and an American General who quietly said to us as we watched the ships leave Brixham, "Well this is it". I was in Brixham when several damaged ships returned two days later. Strangely enough I was standing in exactly the same spot on Berry Head many years later when Berry Head became the property of Torbay Borough and as Vice Chairman of Parks I was involved in the taking-over ceremony. I was then able to mention my other memorable visit.

Earlier in the war I seemed fated to be on leave whenever enemy action took place. To name a few, the bombing of the Palace Hotel, the enemy aircraft shot down on Corbyn beach, the bombing of St Marychurch and various hit and run scares. I was also at the Imperial Hotel when the news of some disaster at Slapton Sands was reported and all servicemen were immediately called away, but it was never made public for security reasons.

I have very happy memories of the Americans who, on the whole, settled so well in what to them was a very strange environment.

FIRE OVER SHALDON

MR R. JACKSON

I was ten years of age at the declaration of the war. Being too young to understand the seriousness of war we thought it was fun. I remember clearly: Mr Chamberlain's speech... also his meeting with Adolf Hitler. Territorials jumping into lorries and off to war. Collections of metal for the war effort, even razor-blades, iron gate railings, saucepans, kettles etc., anything metal.

We lived at Garston Forest, Shaldon at the time. Our gate is still there, it was not taken because there is not a pavement outside. Quite a few bombs fell in Shaldon as well as Teignmouth. I well remember the day Teignmouth Hospital received a direct hit, killing several, including nurses. We children used to explore the wreckage of bombed houses, also collected shrapnel, sometimes still warm from the explosion; other collections included incendiary bombs which occasionally failed to go off, also bullet cases etc. The planes raided frequently, day or night, flying very low at times. I once waved to a German pilot when I stood on a hedge at Labrador. The plane came from Newton Abbot, down the Teign and up through Coombe Valley, so low I was looking from a higher level than the plane, the pilot released a bomb which landed just off shore.

There were many gun sites mostly ack-ack, also pom-poms, and naval guns at the Ness, Shaldon, also a Boom across the mouth of the Teign. Ships had kite balloons to keep off aircraft. Sometimes they broke away; we would watch them fly away and rise until bursting from inside pressure. I made a cape and leggings from balloon fabric. This balloon had been struck by lightning and fell in flames into the river. We were not allowed on the beaches, which were mined and barb-wired against invasion. Roads were tank-trapped also oil-fire trapped. There was great activity when there was an invasion scare.

There was a lot of activity in this area in preparation for invasion. We got on well with the Americans. The "Sea Bees" had occupation of the Sea Breeze Hotel. The Buffs were in the area, also Indian Cavalry in Shaldon. Morgan Giles [boat builders in Teignmouth] built MTBs. We had many evacuees in this area which was supposed to be safer than the city areas. Shaldon senior children travelled to Newton Abbot Highweek School by bus each day.

Dig for Victory: I still use a gardening book supplied by the Royal Horticultural Society, London entitled *The Vegetable Garden Displayed,* with 300 photographs, issued in 1941. The Minister of Fisheries and Food was the Rt Hon R. S. Hudson, the Minister of Food was Lord Woolton. Powdered eggs were much used. All food scraps were saved for pig food. Collecting bins were placed around villages and towns, nothing was wasted in those days.

The Teign House Hotel, Shaldon was half demolished by a bomb. The first bomb on the beach left a large crater which we used to swim in. One bomb dropped from very low level in centre of Shaldon Bowling Green, bounced up over houses and exploded on allotments by Hamiltons, so it actually passed over our house at Garston; a piece of shrapnel stuck into our back door.

The German planes frequently did daylight tip and run raids, flying very low, taking our gunners by surprise, also our men often could not fire for fear of doing damage to us who would be in the line of fire.

I remember the German prison camp, Teignmouth, Milford Park. The prisoners, I believe, were treated very well. Most worked on the land helping with the harvest etc. Also they helped with the construction of the prefabs. Prefabs were constructed in factories and transported by rail. I believe they were intended to last about twenty years, but our family lived in one right up until 1967. We loved them, they were extremely well planned and cosy, usually constructed of aluminium outside and I think asbestos-lined insulation and asbestos inside walls. They had metal cupboards, kitchen units, wardrobes, gas cooker, gas fridge, fireplace in front room with doors fitted and back boiler. We had an outside shed which I believe was intended as an air raid shelter, thick galvanised Nissen-hut shaped, mostly covered by soil. Each dwelling was detached so we all had a hedge and fence - our own private area.

INTO NORMANDY

MR R.C. JOHNS

3 June 1944

H.M.S. *Cattistock*, a hunt class destroyer operating from her base at Sheerness as part of the anti German E boat patrol, received orders to proceed to Portsmouth. Nothing unusual about that. Ship's companies were used to the odd changes of destination without knowing why - the obvious and necessary secrecy of wartime.

I was an electrical artificer at the time, one of a close-knit crew of the usual mixture of regular and hostilities-only ratings. The captain was an R.N. Officer - Lieutenant Keddy, sadly later to be killed on the bridges of *Cattistock* in a post D-Day operation.- but that is another story.

We arrived in Portsmouth rather suprised at the large number of ships crowding the wharfs and anchored off shore. All shore leave was stopped. Swift, re-storing and ammunitioning of our magazine for our twin 4-inch gun and other armaments produced comments of, "Is this it?" "Is this something to do with this second front everyone is hoping for and had been guessing about".

4 June

Something certainly must be happening. Two army officers have come aboard, and we are told by the captain that the ship is now sealed - no one to go ashore and no one to come aboard

The evening of 4 June

All hands on board are mustered in the largest messdeck. The army officers - they smilingly introduced themselves as the FOO and BLO! before revealing that they were a forward observation officer and a bombardment liaison officer. (Jumping ahead a bit - what a wonderful brave part theirs was to be.) Then began something I shall never forget. One of the two officers - I forget which one - told us that the invasion of France, code named Overlord, *would begin tomorrow*.

He then told us what the sequence of events would be. Very early, just after midnight I think he said (my memory doesn't serve me for accurate times I'm afraid) groups of minesweepers would be sweeping lanes across the channel and would continue widening the mine - free stretches for the four thousand odd craft of the invading armada.

Cattistock would sail in the early morning and eventually anchor just off shore of a beach at Arromanches. The name of course meant nothing to us at the time. We would remain there during the initial stages of the invasion. Also in the early hours of the morning there was to be a massive bombing of selected targets by the combined allied air forces. The FOO and BLO would slip ashore when we arrived at Arromanches, and establish themselves, where later they would direct our fire and that of the cruiser *Belfast*, who would be some distance behind us, and the battleship *Rodney* with her mighty guns. Finally in this totally absorbing forecast of events we were given, not just the sequences, but where the armies were expected.

This operation in our sector would be happening in each of the many sectors along the whole of the invasion coast.

Wow! You can imagine the impact on our ship's company when the army officers had concluded their matter-of-fact (but to us mind bending) information. We all dispersed to carry on our jobs trying to take it all in. And this was to start tomorrow.

5 June

As most people know now, the weather on this fateful day started badly, and steadily got worse and it was decided that the operation could not take place. However, as the day wore on with the weather forecast giving little indication of change, the crucial decision was made that tomorrow Operation Overlord would commence regardless.

June 6

We sailed as planned in the very early morning, the going getting rougher as we got out in the Channel - not very pleasant on deck and worse below! But we thought we were better off than the landing craft would be with their shallow draught. There would be quite a lot of soldiers wishing they were on dry land.

Suddenly we heard a distant hum, growing soon to be a mighty roar, of aircraft. Within a few minutes the sky was full of planes, crossing to bomb their targets, coming back from their raid, passing more planes on their way to the targets. Never before had there been such a sight. Our excitement was terrific.

It would not be too much of an exaggeration to say that we could see little of the sky for planes so closely following each other. With retrospective knowledge this was happening across the entire stretch of coast involving the coming invasion. I think I remember it being about three or four o'clock in the morning, but don't pin me down for that detail!

Then a sudden silence except for our own machinery. The last planes had returned home and those of us who had been able to be on deck for this stupendous experience went below to our routine repair and maintenance work. The weather was abating a little and we were making good speed. Our 4-inch guns blasted off quite a few times on the way over, as did escorts of the following landing craft. I'm not sure of the reason, maybe anti-aircraft. I was working below decks until we dropped anchor.

Going up on deck we found the weather was pleasantly calmer We were quite close to an innocent looking beach with a village a little in the distance. We were at Arromanches.

Looking out to sea we could see the large tank landing crafts getting nearer and nearer. What a sight that was! As they approached signals passed between them and us. Soon the first landing craft came as close to the shore as it s draft would allow. Then quite a magic moment for us. It lowered the front ramp and began disgorging its load - tanks of course, but they FLOATED! They couldn't hear us but we cheered like mad - floating tanks! We had wondered why the landing craft had stopped where it did - and how the dickens could the tanks (as we knew them) get ashore? Now we knew.

Soon more and more tank landing craft unloaded and before long there were dozens of tanks chugging to the beach in line abreast.

As each one reached a point where it no longer floated, it stopped and methodically fired shots in a pattern into the sand ahead to explode any planted mines in the path where it would be going. Everything was progressing perfectly.

Then, as we watched the tanks moving forward out of the water - my heart is crying as I write this - there were loud explosions, and I saw three or four of the tanks erupt into flames with no hope at all for the men inside. Tanks continued to land, and eventually after more terrible casualties there were no more incinerations and the army of tanks moved forward with no immediate opposition and forged ahead out of our sight. We were told, much later when evaluations were made overall that, with all the wonderful preparation and meticulous planning, it was not known or expected that attached to the barbed wire coils in the water were some contact mines.

Now the landing crafts packed with soldiers and equipment surged ashore. The wind was rising and many of the craft tossed around with the coxswains straining like mad to keep their craft head on to get to the beach. I saw some of the craft as they neared the beach spun sideways by the wind and waves making the lowering of the ramps hazardous. Some stuck on the sand at various angles, but the soldiers, some of which must surely have been sick with being tossed around, ran down the ramps, quite a few having to jump into the water, all with their heavy packs and their rifles. Quite a lot of the craft made it with a straight run in at the last moment, helped perhaps by a sudden favourable change of wind.

Soon on the beach the soldiers mustered in their units, some assisting their comrades who had been injured by the battering of the landing. I think all of us on board were thinking "Rather you than me mate!" They were just splendid fighting men.

As more and more landed and equipment was sorted out, the units prepared to start inland, following (we assumed) the route of the tanks. Anti aircraft guns must have been set up by our forces along the coast, because after a couple of nights we could see umbrellas of tracer shells continuously through the nights.

Our twin 4-inch was now firing every so often, I assumed as directed by the bombardment liaison officer ashore. Come to think of it, I didn't know when or how our two army officers had got ashore. They were two brave men. I gathered that the aim was hidden German guns, but I can't be sure of that. We could hear the *Belfast's* guns and the mighty *Rodney's* blasting away.

More and more ships were arriving in our area, bringing supplies for the vital follow up of advancing troops.

It was difficult to know just where the first tanks that landed in our section were, but one day, just by sheer luck I and a few other ratings, were on deck just having a break looking at the village and further into the landscape when we saw a wonderful sight, something else I shall never forget. A tank was climbing a mound far in the distance and when it got to the top it turned itself around in a complete circle in a kind of salute and carried on down the other side out of sight.

Quite a few of the landing craft tied up alongside us for a brief spell before carrying on back. The crews of course were glad of some hot soup and snacks from our galley, I wouldn't mind betting that quite a few of our ships company's tots of rum found their way down the welcoming throats of those men; I know mine did!

On D-Day, plus 2 or 3 I can't remember which, we saw much increased activity to seaward of us. Some escorted merchant ships were manoeuvred to be in line, bow or stern. We had no idea why, and even less much later on when we saw on sinking. With all the firing that was going on from our ships to the shore and not seeing any shore to ship firing at that time, we thought somehow that the sinking ship had been hit by a torpedo.

But then another was sinking and another, Of course much much later we learned that this was intentional to create some still water for the beginning of what would be an artificial harbour and port.

Meanwhile two large caissons were being towed to the beach. The weather, after a brief calmer spell, was getting increasingly rough. I can't remember just how long it took but after much arduous, seemingly impossible work one caisson was somehow secured at right angles to the beach and the other joined to it. We guessed that it was going to be a kind of quay, Again, much later we found that this was the first part of what was to be the Mulberry Harbour.

The weather worsened to storm level. Everyone knows now what happened. The following morning, what a sad sight. The second caisson had been broken clear from the first and was on its side a short distance away at an angle, part beached and part in the water. The remaining caisson had been swung around also. Oh, how frustrated must the men have been who had worked, against the odds, and had such rotten luck.

In the days following, the activity to seaward of us increased immensely. We could see very large caissons being towed and, as far as we were able to see, tied up alongside merchant ships. Again, much later on, we know that what we were witnessing was the creation of what was to be Mulberry, the artificial port, and that the old ships we had seen being sunk would be supplemented by these huge caissons to make a kind of breakwater or sea wall.

A few days later we were allowed a brief time ashore, A few of us walked to what we had thought was a small village, but I have found out since that most probably it was the outskirts of a town called Courseulles.

Cattistock was due to leave for Portsmouth soon but we were able to say that we had walked on the soil of what was now part of free France.

THAT FAVOURITE DRESS

MRS D. JOINT

Towards the end of the war, I had a job where the wage was rather low in those days and, until I was a bit older, I had to be contented with what I got. It took perhaps two or three weeks wages to get a frock for 15/- a skirt and/or a pair of everyday shoes. I had spotted a lovely frock and was determined to get it on my next half day off. I went to work clean and respectable enough to get on a lunchtime bus and got to where this dress hopefully still was on the peg. I sorted out my bus fare which was 1/- return then, I think, and off I went. I made straight for the shop, almost afraid the size and colour would be gone. It wasn't. I took it off the peg, asked if I could try it on and it was perfect. I was so pleased and happy to get myself something really nice to wear for best.

The lady who served me folded the dress and packed it neatly whilst I got out my 15/-. "Thank you," she said, "now the next thing I want is your clothing coupon". "Oh," I said, "just a moment". I turned out everything from my handbag, only to find I had left them at home. So no coupons, no dress but money back. I was almost in tears. I would have to wait at least another week before doing the trip again.

However, I did - I remembered my clothing coupons and the same style colour and size dress was still there. I don't know if it was the same one but at least I had something nice to bring home and remember and to keep for a long time - which is more than can be said for thousands of poor people who lost everything.

Then I met two evacuee ladies who came from the Stepney side of London and each had several children. They lived near my family, and I used to fetch their war-time allowances from the nearest post office each week. In return one of them, being a tailoress, altered a brand new coat for me which was far too big and she made a first class job of it. The other lady had been a dressmaker and she made me a pretty dress I'll never forget. Sadly they have passed away now, but I still keep in touch with the youngest sister of the tailoress who lives at Forest Gate and who I traced after about forty years. These are some of the nicest memories the war brought to me, but the many others would take far too long to print. My memory alone had to improve; I had to always remember to take my clothing coupons, along with my identity card, which I still have: number WIPX-79:3.

SCOUTS AT WAR

MR R. KNEEBONE (Living in Devonport, 1942)

My first encounter with the war was as a senior boy scout asssisting civilians to be fitted with gas masks at the Devonport Guildhall. We were asked to assist the Civil Defence in this operation and hundreds of people passed through this centre. At the time I was a young naval shipyard apprentice learning my trade in the Naval Dockyard. I was Devonport born and bred, mostly educated in Devonport and almost without exception found my leisure and entertainment in the town.

When war was declared our scout troop (9th Devonport) was disbanded owing to our headquarters being the Territorial Army hall which was then required full-time by the army. We scouts went our own way, mostly joining the Civil Defence units. I chose the Auxiliary Fire Brigade as a part-timer, our fire station being a small garage at the rear of the shop directly outside the St Levan Road Dockyard gates. We later moved to another garage further along St Levan Road, beneath the railway viaduct. We came later to regret this move owing to the fact that the viaduct was to become a target for the German bombers.

At the outbreak of war the Three Towns fire services were independent of one another and had different screw threads for their fire hydrants so we had to carry adaptors for use in different parts of the city. Eventually the National Fire Service was formed and the universal bayonet fitting made things easier. Our appliance was a Beresford trailer pump which was pulled by a private car and our crew consisted of four teenage males and a mature crew leader. When the heavy raids began we were given leave of absence from work to go full-time as firemen, which lasted two or three weeks. Of course we were then on full fireman's pay.

Most of our fire fighting experience was confined to Devonport, Keyham and Morice Town which we knew well and in which we all lived.

I recall seeing hundreds of soldiers from France, Belgium and Britain sitting on the grass of the Brickfields playing fields after their evacuation from the beaches of Dunkirk, all looking dishevelled and weary. Local people came up and gave them cigarettes etc. through the railings. The Raglan Army Barracks were there at the time and the Brickfield was army land.

In Devonport Park, close to the bowling green, I was in the company of four of my pals when the air raid warning sounded off and almost immediately we saw hundreds of incendiary bombs burning in Mount Edgcumbe Park. We heard the droning of German bombers and we knew we were in for a rough time. I had to go to Morice Square where I lived, to change into my uniform before reporting to my fire station in St Levan Road. My pals were going a different route because they lived in the Pembroke Street area, so we parted company. Very soon afterwards a stick of fire bombs fell across the park and I did not know for a few days that three of my pals had been killed at that time. Also on the way to St Levan Road fire station I was cycling past the Albert Road Gates and saw my first dead bodies lying around near the little park which used to be outside the gates.

From then on life changed dramatically, and I suppose we grew up very quickly. At work we would exchange stories with pals who lived in different parts of the city; some apprentices were in other branches of the civil defence, such as rescue, ambulance and home guard.

There were times when I would be in a dilemma over making a choice of reporting for duty or remaining at home to defend my own home. My older brother was at sea, my younger brother was evacuated to relatives at Chagford, most of the occupants of our block of flats would evacuate town before nightfall, leaving my mother and father plus two or three other occupants on guard. My mother, father and I became very skilful in the use of a dustbin lid, stirrup pump and sandbag. The trick was to stand in the doorway of the corner shop and watch the roof of the block. Any incendiary bombs falling in the street we left alone, but any which fell on the roof were dealt with very quickly indeed.

There was humour sometimes in our activities, such as when my father and I were attempting to extinguish an incendiary bomb in a sofa in a neighbour's first floor flat. We could not completely damp out the fire, so my dad used his axe to remove the window frame, and we then pushed the thing out into the street, where it could burn itself out.

A very sad event was the night when an incendiary bomb fell onto the roof of King Street Senior School where I had spent my early school days. I desperately tried to break into the school, but the doors were very strongly constructed and the ground floor windows were high above the ground level, which made it extremely difficult to enter. I had to leave it because other bombs were threatening my own home, and through the night I watched the school burn to a shell.

An incident which would cause amusement in any other situation was the time a house was burning in the area where the Dockyard Apprentices' Centre now stands. Our appliance had to draw water from a static tank but our hoses had to pass through another house to reach the fire. I was sent to knock on the door and seek permission to lay our hoses through the house. I was confronted with a housewife who was irate at the suggestion of fire hoses on her carpet. She was finally persuaded when we were able to provide rubber-lined hoses which were waterproof. In the meantime all hell was going on round us as the air raid was still in progress.

On another occasion our crew and appliance were required to act as a booster pump to pump water from a static tank outside the Albert Road Gates to an appliance at the crest of the hill near the former Engineering College. We had just started the operation when a shout alerted us to the fact that a land mine suspended from a parachute was rapidly approaching in our direction. We stood with our backs to the Dockyard wall and watched it float over the wall. Suddenly there was a tremendous rush of water down the hill and our pump was swept away towards the Dockyard gates. We could see all this quite clearly because the bombers had dropped flares. We learned afterwards that the mine had exploded in a reservoir inside the wall and had blown the water over the wall into the roadway.

My view of the war at sea was at this time restricted to my work in the Dockyard, and it first hit me when my gang of shipwrights were ordered to dry-dock and repair the bows of H.M.S. *Vanquisher*, a destroyer which had been in collision with a sister ship H.M.S. *Walker*. Apparently some of her ship's company had been trapped in the wreckage and we civvies were not allowed on board until the area had been cleared of human remains and disinfected. Some lorries arrived from the Royal Naval Barracks with some "sailors" equipped with decontamination gear who proceeded to clear away the debris. I put the term sailors in inverted commas because the "sailors" were only partly dressed in uniform. They had only arrived to join the navy the day before and had not even completed their uniform issue. What an introduction to things to come!

TORQUAY HIT AND RUN

MRS M. LAWRENCE

In August 1942 I came home to my parents for a holiday before taking my final nursing exams. I had two friends with me and my brother was also on leave at the time. On this day, I think it was the 24th, we set out for a picnic and a walk along the cliffs along Bishop's Walk. When we reached the point below the Marine Drive we decided it was time for lunch, and climbed up to an open grassy glade between the Walk and below the Marine Drive, overlooking the cliffs and the sea.

We heard the sound of planes but could not see any in the sky above. Then suddenly we saw three planes below us, low on the sea, coming towards us at great speed. They flew up and went right over our heads, not more than a few yards from us and we saw the pilots quite clearly. No doubt they saw us too. They flew inland and then we heard three explosions, one after the other. Then, a little further up the coast towards Babbacombe, we saw these three fighters speeding back down to sea level again.

There were two or three little rowing boats off the coast at this point, we saw them quite clearly being machine-gunned by these planes, we could see the line of bullets straddling the boats. We decided that we had better go home to see what had happened. Our home was at the Manor Road end of Cary Park and as we approached we saw that a bomb had been dropped on the Tennis Courts in the Park. We met our neighbour who was an A.R.P Warden at the time and he was in a very excited state. He assured us that our house was not hit but a bomb had fallen on the small row of houses behind us on the corner of Warbro Road, completely demolishing them and killing the people at home, but leaving "The Fortunes of War" intact, and there it still stands.

Our house suffered only from the blast. My father, enjoying his apples and custard for his lunch found a plate of broken glass before him, and his garden covered with broken bricks and other debris.

We learned afterwards that these fighters were Fokke-Wulfs, with fixed machine guns. Had they been Messerschmitts they could have shot us where we were sitting. The small boats on the sea had in them patients from the Palace Hotel RAF Hospital, and we heard that one man had been killed and others wounded.

This was just one of the 142 hit and run raids on Torquay. My brother painted a little picture of this scene, with Hope's Nose and cliffs below us on the right and the wing of a German plane over our heads. A very good memento of this occasion.

THE SPIRIT OF DEVONPORT

MRS PEARL AUDREY MERRETT (nee WHITE)

Memories of the Plymouth/Devonport blitz still haunt me to this day. We resided at 3 Cross Street Devonport. Our street fronted onto the back of Alhambra Theatre. My thoughts go back to the sirens alerting us to the start of an air-raid. Then the terrible droning noise of the enemy bombers above us. The anxious moments we all had as we made our way to the nearest air-raid shelter when we saw the bombs and incendiary devices exploding and lighting up the darkness not knowing if we would live or die.

My father was in the Home Guard Service. Many a time when we were all rushing for shelter my father would take it in turns to carry the elderly piggy-back fashion to get them safely to the air-raid shelter.

One of the shelters I remember we used was situated beneath Devonport Market. I read an account of the Blitz in a newspaper in the past couple of years to the effect that this shelter had received a direct hit by the enemy during the Blitz. I remember that we also used the air-raid shelter situated beneath Devonport Park.

One day all the families in our street were told to leave there houses because a very large undetonated bomb had landed at the bottom of the street. We never again saw our houses or effects because the bomb eventually went off, demolishing everything around the locality. I remember that my dad had gone to a lot of trouble to make me a doll's house for Christmas 1940, and I have never forgotten at how upset I was over its loss in the Blitz.

My primary school, York Street, was situated about 150 yards from my home, and again I can remember how upset I was when we all saw it go up in smoke and flames and razed to the ground.

I can recollect that the day after and air-raid my brother and I would go into the streets to pick up pieces of shrapnel, which would still be warm to the touch. I remember too, all the barrage balloons way up in the sky, doing a worthwhile job.

My dad used to spend a lot of time during the raids on duty, to see what assistance he could give in any way with casualities, etc. The ARP would always be on duty.

After our home was destroyed, a friend of the family invited us to her house, to use two rooms for the time being. This house was situated a few yards away from the Western Hotel, Fore Street, which was just across the road from the Forum Cinema, which still stands to this day. I have vivid memories of one night when my mother told my brother, sister and me, who had just gone off to sleep, to slip our coats over our pyjamas as the siren had sounded the warning of an air-raid, and we had to rush to Devonport Park shelter.

I remember how frightened we all were as we rushed along Fore Street to the shelter; I happened to glance back as bombs and incendiary devices were being dropped and lighting up the darkness as if it were daylight, due to the explosions and fires caused by them. There was a strong smell of burning and the heavy smoke everywhere. I could see the house we had left some moments before going up in flames, and to this day I can't help feeling how lucky we were to come through the war.

What a big relief it was when we reached the safety of the shelter in Devonport Park, where we went down steps to join man other families until the siren sounded the all clear! I can remember trying to go to sleep on the wooden benches amongst the sound of everyone's voices. We all used to sing the popular songs of the day to keep our spirits up. e.g. "It's A Long Way to Tipperary", "Pack up Your Troubles", "Lily of Laguna", "Underneath the Arches", etc.

I had an Aunt and Uncle, Mr and Mrs A Herring who lived in a flat in a big house near the railway station at Exmouth Road, Stoke, Devonport. They did not like going to the air-raid shelter but preferred to stay underneath the stairs when a raid occurred . The German bombers were trying to bomb the railway station but my aunt and uncle lost their lives through a direct hit on their house.

Only grown-ups were allowed to visit the Efford Cemetery for the mass funeral of the civilian war dead, totalling nearly 400 persons. I remember that when my father and mother and other relations were going to the cemetery that I wanted to go with them as I had loved my late aunt and uncle very much.

I also remember when we had to travel by bus with many people to Plympton, where we used to use a Church Hall for sleeping purposes. We used to have blankets to sleep on, and the floor would be full of people, I can still see the big churns that they used to feed us soup from. I remember that because we only had the clothes that we wore, we were taken to another Church, Sherwell Church, North Hill, where we went into the Hall where we were fitted with clothes and shoes.

I know I was only six years old but I have vivid recollections of the camaraderie which existed amongst the Devonport folk. Everybody seemed to help each other, and do good turns for one another. For a short while we resided at 16 Edinburgh Road, Devonport, the home of my aunt and uncle: Mr and Mrs W Earnshaw, their family and my granddad (they had a flat there). This road was situated right next to the Dockyard.

When the American soldiers came to Devonport they were situated in huts not far from Edinburgh Road. All of us children used to go and see them, they would hand us gifts of chocolate and chewing gum. I can remember when they would join with us in a game of baseball. Not long afterwards we were allocated a flat in a house at Vanguard Villas, Keyham, Devonport, which was near the Royal Naval Barracks. This was only temporary, because the owners were evacuated.

The owners came back to claim their home, so we had another move to Walters Road, St Budeaux, Plymouth. Not far away in Normandy Way there were more huts which housed many American sailors. I was never told at the time what these servicemen were doing in Devonport and St Budeaux, It was only recently that I became aware of how these servicemen and many more Americans joined with our Armed Forces in the D-Day landings in 1944 in Normandy.

THE LONGEST DAY

MR J.T. NEWTON

As D-Day approached, we were moved to the troop concentration areas around Portsmouth, where every roadside was lined with tanks and vehicles parked nose to tail for mile after mile. I had never seen such a concentration of transport.

I remember being surprised to receive our pay in francs, on the last pay day before embarking (notes printed especially for the troops).

We embarked on 2 June ready for the invasion originally planned for 4 June, but postponed due to bad weather in the Channel. Our accommodation from then until the morning of 6 June was an assortment of landing craft. I was one of the lucky ones, on a L.S.T (Landing Ship Transport) carrying tanks and other vehicles.

During the waiting in the Channel we had to find whatever shelter we could in or under the vehicles, which were mostly full of stores. In the L.S.T there were a few bunks in the areas designated for personnel, but not nearly enough room for all, and in our vessel, the Canadians were first to board, so we didn't get a look in. Most of the leisure time during the wait was taken up learning from the Canadians how to play crap (dice) and then joining in to gamble our francs. The Canadians were a great bunch of fellows. In the actual crossing we sailed past a floating mine. Shots were directed at it, but without success. We hoped it would not come into contact with any of the many craft behind us.

Our company supported the Berkshire Infantry Regiment and we were attached to the 3rd Canadian Division. We formed No. 8 Beach Group and it was our job to clear the beaches and surrounding areas of obstructions, mines and booby traps to enable supplies to be off-loaded and stored. We started landing shortly after H-Hour on D-Day and continued until we were all ashore.

We landed on Nan Section of JUNO beach at Bernières-sur-Mer. The L.S.T had large doors in the bow and towed alongside it a huge metal raft, known as a "Rhino". Due to size, weight and load the ship grounded well short of the waterline. The Rhino, driven by a system of outboard motors was brought to the front of the ship and with the doors open the transport was driven onto it. When loaded, the Rhino was then propelled to the beach. I said earlier that I was one of the lucky ones, because I was able to cadge a lift on the roof of one of our trucks, which meant that I didn't get my feet wet, a valuable consideration as it was almost a week before I was able to remove my boots for any length of time.

Assault craft were everywhere and vehicles littered the beach above and below water level. As we travelled up the beach, three or four of us on the roof of one vehicle, a German plane approached, travelling along the line of the beach. Bombs could be seen clearly below it. We leaped to the ground and the bombs passed over the truck and exploded a short distance up the beach to our right. Then the journey continued to our designated area. German prisoners were put into beached assault craft. I remember thinking what a hard and grim lot they looked.

The 6 June has been described as the 'Longest Day". For me the day went quickly, but the night was certainly the longest ever. At the end of the day when our work was done and we had established our company lines, I managed to dig myself a trench partly covered with a sheet of steel (discarded waterproofing from a tank) and a few inches of sand. I virtually fell into my trench and into a deep sleep only to be woken and told to report for duty. I was much refreshed and rather surprised when I discovered I had been asleep for just over one hour!

TRAGEDY AT TORQUAY

MRS E. PATTERSON

I have a very special war-time memory, which will live with me until I die.

I had already been through the dreadful Coventry Blitz, where I had been sent from Brixham to go on munitions, this was 1941.

In May 1943 I came home to Brixham to nurse my sick mother, by then I had married and had a baby of 8 months. We lived at Number 5, Greens Court, Higher Street. The Courtyard had six cottages, which had a wall about six feet, where we could stand and look down to the harbour, across the bay, and out to Berry Head. It was a peaceful quiet Sunday morning, sunny, and so calm, the time was about 10.45 am.

A few neighbours, myself, baby, and brother, were gazing down at the harbour, when the peace was broken by the loud drone of planes. We could not believe what we were seeing: six planes, so low, they seemed to skim the water, were making for Torquay. My brothers said, "My God, they are low" never dreaming they were not ours. The next minute we knew differently; the dreadful "thud-thud" of bombs which were all too familiar to me.

I raced indoors clutching my little one, ran upstairs crying, "Mam, Mam, what can I do?" I knew she was too ill to be moved, and I shall never forget her reply. She said, "Hurry to number three, they have a Morrison shelter, you will be safe there. Don't worry about me, I am going to die anyway".

I did hurry to number three, but I just could not leave my mother alone, so I went back to her. Thank God, within minutes the all clear sounded, but the Germans had done their cruel work, a bomb had fallen on St Marychurch, Torquay and killed 21 little children as they were at Sunday School, this was 30 May, Rogation Sunday, 1943.

My dear Mam died in July.

SOUTH HAMS EVACUATION

MRS P. D. REEVE

I was just ten when the announcements were made. All parishioners were called to the Parish Church at Stokenham, in the middle of November 1944, to be told they would have to leave their homes, their villages, their farms - all within six weeks. This was because the beaches and countryside at Slapton Sands closely resembled beaches in Normandy, and it would greatly help the American troops to practice seaborne landings before attempting to invade France and force the Germans out. The parishioners were not told too much about this purpose, because it had to be kept from German intelligence, although the evacuation was a subject of Pathe News at the time.

I do not remember being told about this approaching upheaval. Our parents would have gone to the meeting, and told us children the next day. They joined with mother's sister and her three daughters, all older than us three, and daddy's brother, sister and aunt, and found a large house in Torquay to share. It was called Mount Warren, in St Lukes Road North, and they joked about it being a rabbit warren with all of us there.

People had to find their own accommodation, but they received government help with the actual move. Many farmers had to sell or slaughter their animals. Some managed to move in with relatives outside the evacuation area. My parents had a poultry farm, and all the chickens had to be slaughtered. They probably were sold for food, but I have no recollection of this. We were at school of course, and would not have been aware of all the hustle and bustle the grown-ups were involved in. I do remember the batteries and other equipment was removed to a large barn somewhere near Buckfastleigh . A team of sailors was provided to help with this operation. It took several days. Mummy felt she should provide them with a hot meal at midday, but our rations would not stretch to feeding them, and there were no chickens or eggs available. So she made a large pan of boiled onions in milk, and served it with potatoes and bread. Bread was not then rationed as far as I can recall. There was one sailor who said he didn't like onions, but I am sure he ate the meal and found it very tasty. Their officer gave our dad a plug of navy tobacco, and a bottle of rum, which greatly delighted him. He had served on destroyers in the Great War, and always looked on himself as a naval man. My brother was allowed to travel on the lorry up to Buckfastleigh, but we girls had to stay at home.

We had a dolls' house, a replica of the real one we lived in. The builder was a family friend and had made it for us. We had to leave it behind for lack of space at Torquay. The house had been smashed to pieces when we returned.

We returned one day in late November, about three weeks before the end of term. there had been some damage to our house - bayonets seemed to have been pushed into the ceiling, and the door handles had been stolen. My parents felt rather bitter about this, because the replacement handles were of lesser quality.

It must have been difficult obtaining vegetables for everyone at that time, because none had been grown the previous summer, except perhaps for a few self-sown ones. I recall my mother picking young stinging nettles to provide a green vegetables for us, but we did not appreciate this too well, and she did not do it a second time. She must have been very busy without that sort of thing to do.

My father had difficulty re-starting the poultry farm. He needed a ration for the chickens' feed, and it was difficult to provide sufficient food for them, even when we had re-stocked. Rats had multiplied throughout the evacuation area, and he used gins to trap them on our land. For some reason I took it upon myself to help him in this task, and would beat on the head with a stick any trapped rats that were not already dead. There were many rats in the corn ricks that autumn. Binders were still used for harvesting, and the corn had to be stored in ricks until it could be threshed. Chasing the fleeing rats was great sport for dogs and children.

Our friends in the village who had returned earlier had roamed the fields, occasionally finding articles the soldiers had left behind. Tins of hash were among these treasurers. They were often heated up on camp fires to make a tasty picnic, though our mother said it would be better if we brought any such finds home to supplement the family rations. On one occasion a younger boy, a farmer's son, and his friend found a live shell. Unfortunately they handled it, and the farmer's son was killed.

Sometimes we would wander as far as Stokeley. on the inner edge of Torcross Ley. The Americans had built a footbridge across the Ley, and we would, of course, walk over this. It was somewhat rickety, and our mother implored us not to use it. She was very relieved when it was removed.

During the year in Torquay I should have taken the scholarship exam, but did not because we went to the private school. On our return to Stokenham my father asked Devon County Council if I could take it a year late, which they agreed to. My sister and I, therefore, took this exam at the same time, and consequently we both were in the same form at Kingsbridge Grammar School throughout our subsequent schooling.

Most of the sea defences had been removed during the evacuation, so we could use the beach at Torcross again. We were not allowed to go very far up beside the line because of the danger of mines remaining buried in the shingle. Eventually they were cleared, but for many years mines were still occasionally uncovered and would have to be detonated under control.

BUDLEIGH HOSPITALITY

MR H. R. RICE Jr

I was in command of 'L' Company, 3rd Battalion, 12th Infantry. My Company Headquarters was in a home on a street off the main street, going away from the Channel, and curving to the right. If I recall correctly this street was east of the street going toward the Channel to the Rosemullion Hotel. The pub on the lower level, or basement, of the Rosemullion was reserved for officers and nearly every night we would congregate there for our iced lagers and dart games.

The Battalion Headquarters was, as I recall it, in a home on a hill further north of my company headquarters. Our battalion commander often invited local dignitaries to Sunday breakfast at the officer's mess there. Seeing how these dignitaries relished these breakfasts made us realise how much better we were fed that the local citizenry.

Our stay in Budleigh Salterton was most pleasant for both officers and men. Without prompting from higher authority everyone did their best to prove to the local population that we were truly professional 'spit and polish' soldiers. I can't recall a single incident (although there must have been some) where our men ran foul of the local peace officers or with local citizens. I felt that there was a mutual respect between us. It did become obvious to many of us that it must have been a time of considerable sacrifice for the local citizens who gave up their homes, favourite pubs, etc. for us. However, never did I receive a complaint or even a disapproving look. We only received their smiles and best wishes, which we did our best to return.

In June 1988 my wife and I were on a bus tour of the UK. During a stopover in Plymouth we hired a car and driver and revisited Budleigh Salterton for a few hours. I could not find the old Battalion Headquarters at all. I am sure that I narrowed down my Company Headquarters to one of three homes. I had no trouble at all finding the Rosemullion, which was being converted into apartments. I had a difficult time explaining to my wife why the only place I could definitely remember was the pub.

We had lunch at a pub on the main street and I asked where I might find someone old enough to remember our visit in 1944. No one could help me. But my returning to Budleigh Salterton was still the highlight of our tour for me. I ask that all citizens of Budleigh Salterton old enough to remember us, accept my thanks for all that was done to welcome us and make us 'feel at home' while we were there. I will never forget your smiles and friendliness that hid the strain, suffering and inconvenience the war and we Yanks caused you.

RESCUE AT DUNKIRK

MR R. SMITH (Tamerton Foliot)

I was a member of Monty's 3rd Infantry Division. We were falling back to Dunkirk. My platoon with Bren gun carriers were ordered to hold the main crossroads onto La Panne until approximately twelve midnight when the last vehicle would be the Medical Officer's, then to make our own way to Dunkirk after destroying our vehicles.

We came under mortar fire and lost three men but held the position until three a.m. Instead of destroying the vehicles we used them to see if we could get through La Panne, but we were unable to get through the town. There was fire all along the streets with burned out vehicles and wires criss-crossing all over the place. We had to leave our Bren gun carriers, not without a grenade near the engine. I told the men, "This is it, make your own way along the beach." You could see Dunkirk from the fires of ships and the red glow in the sky from the town.

Dawn found us on the sand dunes of La Panne. There were three of us in our group but thousands on the beach and forming queues into the water where the navy boys were coming in with small boats picking up as many as they could.

Then the bombers came in - Stukas dive-bombing the queues. We were watching as the bombs dropped into the men. The ranks closed up where the crater was. It was hellish. We couldn't stay in the dunes, so had to take our chance in the water. There was a destroyer laid off about 300 yards. I said we could swim to her but Darkie, our chum, said, "You two go ahead. I can't swim." We said, "We'll take you with us. Just hang onto a plank of wood, you'll be okay." He wouldn't have agreed but fighter planes came along very low and started machine-gunning the troops in the water, killing many. At last we had him on a large bit of wood, part of a hatch cover. We were doing well - half way there - when five Stukas attacked the ship and nearly blew her out of the water.

So it was back to the dunes. Later in the day we found a motor-boat well up on the beach. It was undamaged. I said "Do you think the engine will work?" After checking around we found the engine was okay; all we wanted was petrol. That was no bother as there were scores of vehicles all along the beach.

We worked to clear the sand from behind the boat so that the tide would come up to float her. She was about 22 feet long. There were some black French troops dug in near the boat. The officer spoke a little English and we told him that we intended to try to sail the boat to England. He said "You'll have to wait about six hours for the tide, so have something to eat and drink, but we only have roast potatoes and wine." They were burnt black but tasted great after so long without food.

As we were watching the incoming tide a batch of bombers came along the beach. One turned back dropping a stick of bombs which blew our boat to bits.

On the last day of the evacuation we made our way along the mole at La Panne. It was about 3a.m. Ships were burning and the mole was pitted with craters. I thought we would never make it. Near the end of the mole I saw a British helmet rise over the side and then he shouted, "Anyone for the Skylark?" I crawled along and he said, "You're lucky, we were just going to push off." It was a small trawler with a two man crew. The skipper said, "We can't use the engine, so push along the mole with your hands, and if any of you know your prayers, start saying them." They were pouring everything in to stop craft getting in and leaving.

There were about 120 men on that boat; you could hit the water with your hand easily. We were lucky and after a while we heard the skipper shout, "Okay Geordie, start her up, and get the hell out of here!" When I came to we were unloading in Swansea, Wales.

I was also involved in the landings at Arromanches; that was a picnic compared to Dunkirk.

AIRBORNE INVADER

MR R. STUDDEN

In the late Spring of 1943 I joined 6th Airborne Division as a radio operator following earlier training in basic infantry skills and specialist courses on signals equipment. The Division was then being formed with a small cadre of regular members but with a major proportion of conscripted men. We had chosen to serve in an airborne unit for a variety of reasons - every member of my unit was a volunteer.

On or about 2 June 1944 our final in-depth briefing for Overlord, the invasion of Normandy. 6th Airborne Division's role was to seize and hold land East of the River Orne and its parallel canal. The plans had several vital objectives and included the seizure of the bridge (Pegasus Bridge) before the enemy could detonate the charges known to be in place. The assault on a heavy gun battery at Merville whose guns could command the invasion beaches. The guns had to be silenced before any troops landed from the sea.

Our flight was uneventful. Anti-aircraft fire as we neared the French coast was we were told, about the usual intensity. We suffered no casualties. Shortly after midnight we left the aircraft. We were lucky. Our navigator had identified our DZ (dropping zone) and I was unable to see the river and the canal during the short period of descent. Pale moonlight did not assist in identifying the church tower and I landed in France with no clear idea of in which direction any rendezvous lay.

I gathered up the contents of my kit bag, a padded container which I jumped with strapped to one leg, established the radio equipment was intact and set off for Ranville using starlight as a guide. Within minutes of landing I came upon a colleague stumbling around only semi-conscious. He had collided with a high stone wall on landing - suffering superficial injuries and concussion. Small arms fire was erupting around us accompanied by occasional rounds of artillery and mortar fire.

We set off for Ranville and were soon joined by a motley collection of other divisional troops scattered on landing. Our progress was as rapid as circumstances allowed. As number increased we became a more effective fighting unit but we became involved in small skirmishes and suffered our first casualties. I vividly recall the sound of German horse-drawn transport rattling through the deep cut Normandy lanes.

Some hours after daylight and almost within sight of our RV we heard the sound of bagpipes - almost surreal in the circumstances. Coming towards us along the main road came lines of green berets! Led by a kilted piper marching along the centre of the road with the Commando leader Lord Lovatt. The first sea-borne landings had succeeded and we had linked up. So far so good.

EVACUEE

MR M. SWAIN

My memories begin with leaving Waterloo Station on Sunday 3 September for my longest train journey, with my younger brother. I had my 11th birthday at Easter, but he would not be nine until the middle of November. We had been prepared for a few weeks. First, the brown boxes with the funny gas-masks had come to School, which was not far from the Old Kent Road, in Walworth. Then the 'trying-on' lessons. We had to carry them, as well as our small leather suitcases. I have a vague memory of a larger black canvas bag, all marked with our names, and lot of labels.

We arrived at Hayward's School, opposite the old red stone Crediton Church, in afternoon sunshine, to be met by groups of ladies. Some were young, dressed similar to nurses, others, who were members of the WVS, in green uniform.

Our final destination was Newton St Cyres. We had never seen whitewashed cottages before, and certainly not the friendly village dairyman, Mr Coles, who was the father of our first lady guardian. We were taken to our new home, a house with a garden and garage, near the Station.

In a few days we went to the village school, but I was soon to leave my brother behind, and move to Crediton. I had been given a grammar school place, having passed the scholarship exam, and to find out that I was 'our evacuee'.

My new guardians lived in a roomy house, in the High Street, with an old courtyard at the back. I had my own room, with a view over the fields above the town. There was also a black cat, called Peter. The landlord, who lived next door, was a retired wheelwright, but who had lost a leg in the Great War. However, he was able to travel and walk quite long distances, with a great store of knowledge. He had made a wall sundial, which hung below my window.

Another early country memory returns, of a school trip to Torrington Moor to pick 'teddies', and for which we earned several shillings!

The helpful ladies of the WVS organised some of us into groups to help with the war effort. One task was the collection of salvage, usually waste-paper. One or two had joined the scouts, and we went about with the large wooden cart to collect bundles.

The wartime pattern changed, with the arrival of soldiers, some being billeted locally. I think most of them belonged to the Royal Signals, and came from northern counties. Later, the Senior Medical Officer, (RAMC), garaged his car in one of the landlord's buildings, next to one reserved for the local veterinary surgeon.

Our local unit was enlarged by some of the survivors from the Dunkirk evacuation. I believe some of these had kept the distinctive cap-badge of the Gloucesters. When the schoolboys had reached the age of twelve it was time to join the Corps, later to become a detachment of the Army Cadet Force, and attached to a reserve unit of the Devons. The Headmaster held a reserve rank of Lieut Colonel, supported by younger officers from the staff, soon to leave for active service. The School Company was noted for its band, and was trained by a very experienced local musician.

We had seen a red glow in the western sky, during the winter nights, but worse was to come. Then the skies were lit up by fires, as well as the continued echoes of gunfire. Plymouth was to become the "worst hit city" by the middle of 1941. Some of the local fire-crews worked at the factory, where my guardian was foreman. We were told of their duty calls to as far away as Bristol.

BOMBS OVER THE CITY

MR T. TREVAIL

On the night of Saturday 12 and Sunday 13 June 1943, I woke to the mournful wail of the siren. Mother had shaken us out of our sleep and, with urgency in her voice, started to dress us. "Come on, we've got to hurry, the German planes are coming." I sat on the bed and started to doze off again. We all ran downstairs and into the cool night air, keeping close to the reservoir wall as we ran to our shelter which was next to the ARP wardens' shelter. Mother carried baby John in one hand and held the respirator in the other. My brother and sister had our gas masks slung over our shoulders attached to string in a cardboard box.

We reached the shelter in a couple of minutes and slammed the reinforced concrete door. The muffled sound of the siren sent shivers down our spines. Soon afterwards the night sky was made like day as an enemy pathfinder aircraft dropped flares. A little later a force of about twenty bombers came in over the city. My father John was in the ARP shelter with the other wardens. Bombs came raining down on the city as before and the explosions were terrible; the ground shook with each onslaught. The Bofors gun in the back lane was pounding away and the already bright night sky was lit up with tracer bullets from all over the city. Suddenly a shout went went up with one accord from the wardens' post, "He's been hit... he's been hit. Hurrah!"

My elder sister Jean and I opened the huge door between us and shouted to father, wanting to see what had been hit. He beckoned us out, pointing to the sky, and there, caught in the beam of a searchlight, was an enemy bomber, huge tongues of flame belching from the fuselage. Mother stayed put in the safety of the shelter. The plane was heading towards Dartmoor but as we continued to watch it swung round 180 degrees and came straight for us, getting lower and lower all the time. Father shouted, "It's going to hit us!" and grabbing us both he ushered us back inside the shelter, against our protestations. We heard the plane roar overhead at about 100 feet and a few seconds later we heard the terrific explosion as it crashed in the garden of a house that was being used by the WRNS in Penlee Way.

Within minutes some of the wardens were on their way to see whether there would be any survivors from the wreck. Rene Lamble, an ARP warden, suffered badly from arthritis in her legs and was way behind the others, and when she did arrive she went into the garden where bullets were whizzing around from the plane. "Get out Rene you'll get your head shot off!" a warden shouted. Arthritis or not, she moved out of danger so quickly they said later that she beat the speed record for the hundred yard dash!

The plane was a Junkers 88 bomber, and just before it met its destruction, one of the crew baled out and fell into the trees, his parachute failing to open. The rest of the crew were killed where they sat, and in the horrendous heat there was nothing anyone could do.

The RAF and the local police were quickly on the scene, as well as the AFS, and cordoned off the area. When father returned some hours later we wanted to know all about it. I could just imagine all that shrapnel lying around and made up my mind that at the earliest possible moment I would try to get some. The next morning mother was getting my two sisters and me ready for Sunday school. We always wore our Sunday best clothes and, as a seven year old, I was fidgeting as she dressed me in my light brown serge jacket and trousers (which came down just below my knees), my hob nailed boots and long stocking. "For goodness sake keep still Tony. You have never been in a hurry to go to Sunday school before. What's up with you!".

PLYMOUTH INFERNO

MRS V. VINCENT

I cannot forget an experience I had during the bombing of Plymouth. I was employed by the Western National Bus Company, being one of the first three conductors employed in Plymouth.

I was on duty the first night of the Plymouth Blitz. My bus was the Newton Ferrers and Noss Mayo run and I was due to leave the City Centre at 6.00pm. At ten minutes to six my bus was full ready to go (a duplicate would follow). I approached a stand inspector and said, "I am full, I cannot carry any more". I had over twenty standing on a single decker bus. "Can I go?" He said, "No Blondie, (that was their name for me then) if you leave ten minutes early and should there be an accident of any kind, you will be for the high jump". Within that ten minutes, which would be 6.00p.m., the sirens sounded, and everyone had to go to a shelter.

Myself and many other conductors went to the basement in the office. Continuous bombing went on around us for many hours, Plymouth was an absolute inferno. Next to the Western National Office was a YMCA with, I'm sure, many servicemen which received a direct hit. Next door an Italian cafe was bombed flat also. We were still below wondering if we would be next. Everything, everywhere was one mass of flames with nearly every building flattened. Many of our buses on the stand were also blown up.

A driver, I cannot remember his name, had the presence of mind to fill up the bus with conductors and drivers and, after hours of continuous bombing, he drove through Plymouth, chancing his life and ours, to take us to the Mount Gold Hospital. I was given a couple of tablets for shock and finally, we nearly all passed out. I often wonder how many of the passengers there were in my bus survived as this was the first night of the Plymouth blitz.

I remember our Queen had visited Plymouth that same afternoon and I turned to my driver and said, "I bet we will get it tonight", as I'm sure previously our Queen visited Coventry which was heavily bombed just after her visit there. I do hope my passengers on that fateful night, the first night of the Plymouth blitz, survived to tell the tale.

ASSAULT ON EXETER

The Countess Wear Bridges and the British 6th Airborne Division airborne assault in Normandy on 6th June 1944

COLONEL DAVID J. WOOD M.B.E.

I was a platoon commander in letter "D" or Major Howard's Company, 2nd Battalion Oxfordshire and Buckinghamshire Light Infantry, when, in April 1944, after two years of solid training and a near miss for the Sicily invasion, it became increasingly clear that something was in the wind. As evidence of this we saw much more than our share of VIPs - always an ominous sign - my company commander disappeared at frequent intervals, returning with a knowingly secret look and, perhaps most significantly of all, we suddenly started finding previously precious transport much easier to get and German uniforms and weapons, on which we had to train, began to arrive.

Although we did not know either where we were going into action or exactly what our role was going to be, it was obvious to all ranks that we had been selected for a special task of some kind. We carried out dry rehearsals with two "bridges" taped on flat ground above our camp at Bulford *ad nauseam*, by day and by night, employing every conceivable combination of tasks - a wise precaution, as it turned out.

It soon became obvious to those planning the subsequent operation that we needed to find a real location which, as far as possible, more closely resembled our still top secret and vital objective on D-Day. Some diligent staff work discovered the two bridges at Countess Wear and on 21 May 1944, what later became known as the Coup de Main Assault Party consisting of six glider borne platoons of infantry and a party of sappers (Royal Engineers), moved down to Exminster to begin a period of three days and nights of intense military activity in the area of the Countess Wear Bridges over the River Exe and the Exeter Canal.

There, we carried out a seemingly endless, complicated and very noisy series of rehearsals, attacking the two bridges from different directions, using a variety of permutations in an attempt to find a simple plan which would cater for every eventuality. It was a very tiring experience and we were all sick of the sight of the two bridges and the "enemy" who manned them when, on the last evening, the men were paid a day early and let loose on the unsuspecting city of Exeter.

Some drank too much and damage was done to more than one window. It took a personal approach by my company commander (a former police officer himself) and an understanding senior police officer (with First World War medal ribbons) to get everyone back to camp without charges being preferred.

On 26 May the assault party moved to a secure transit camp at Tarrant Rushton. There we were joined by twelve very experienced pilots from the Glider Pilot Regiment who had already practised navigating and landing our Horsa gliders by day and by night more than fifty times, on a piece of ground which resembled our eventual landing zone in Normandy. Both officers and men were briefed on our operation from an incredibly accurate model of the area around what later became known as the Pegasus and Horsa Bridges over the Canal de Caen and the River Orne. Every house, pill-box, slit trench and tree on our landing zone was shown - we even knew the names of the café proprietors near the canal bridge and the fact that he spoke English.

Our orders were crystal clear: "to seize intact the bridges over the River Orne and Caen Canal at Ranville and Bénouville and hold until relieved". If the bridges had been demolished we were to establish posts on either bank. We were to land at 00.20 hours on D-Day, with three platoons attacking each bridge and its defences. The sappers had the unenviable task of locating and removing demolition charges from each bridge. Each glider would carry two pilots, 25 infantry and sappers, an assault boat and bangalore torpedoes (for blowing up the wire defences). Recognition in the dark was to be achieved by shouting a code-word and success signals included the words "ham" and "jam" on the radio or victory "V" sounded on the OC's whistle. At the conclusion of the orders, the men asked one question: "Could we have our own medical officer?" This was quickly arranged and Captain John Vaughan RAMC who, unlike the rest of us had never flown in a glider, joined us the next day.

The aerial reconnaissance photographs provided by the RAF, from which we were briefed, were regularly up-dated. It came as something of a shock to learn from some of the later ones that numerous white dots, which could be either anti-landing poles or holes, had appeared on our landing zones. Our intrepid glider pilots assured us that, although the poles were staggered and it would be dark when we landed, they would have no trouble steering their aircraft through them. Such was our faith in the pilots that we actually believed them! (Thank goodness, we found on landing that the poles had not yet been placed in the holes dug for them.).

We were issued with a variety of special items of escape equipment, ranging from magnetic fly buttons which could make a simple compass, silk map of France, a small metal file to be concealed in our battledress collars and, in the case of the officers, about £30 of French francs with which to buy ourselves out of trouble.

On Sunday 4 June there was a false alarm. We were warned to go that night but when preparations, viz the move to the airfield, were almost complete, the operation was postponed. The sense of disappointment was overwhelming and my diary records the fact that an unusually large amount of whisky was consumed that night, in an attempt to drown our sorrows.

The next day it was the real thing. We test fired our weapons for the umpteenth time, primed our grenades, blacked our faces, ate a "fat free" meal to prevent air sickness and moved to the airfield where we emplaned in our gliders for take-off. Major Howard came round to wish us all good luck, the sliding doors were shut, we fastened our seat belts and waited.

We took off at one-minute intervals between 2256 and 2301 hours, towed behind Halifaxes which flew onto bomb targets in France, in order to conceal our intentions. The flight took about one hour and fifteen minutes during which we sat strapped in facing each other rather like the seats in an old-fashioned tram. We sang at first but kept silent later - I think we feared the enemy might hear us. I went to the rear of the glider once to check the tail and parachute when someone reported that it had moved but I could not - luckily - find anything wrong and returned to my seat, making reassuring noises to my men.

We cast off at about 6-7,00 feet over the coast of Normandy and "glid" for about seven minutes. It was an eerie feeling, swishing silently through the night with the fields clearly visible through the doors which we had opened to ensure a quick exit. Quite suddenly, one of the pilots shouted, "Christ, there's the bridge!" and we were descending for a rough and bumpy landing at about 90 m.p.h. with the skids throwing up sparks from flints in the ground - we thought they were sounds of enemy tracer and that we were already under fire! The impact of the landing broke the glider's back and I was pitched out through the plywood side - I was never more glad that I was not travelling in American WACOs with their steel frames.

I collected my platoon and pushed forward to the barbed wire fence into which no. 1 glider had crashed its nose - a wonderful piece of piloting. I reported to John Howard and moved across the road to start my task of clearing the inner defences. No. 1 platoon had silenced the pill-box and rushed across the canal bridge which providently did not blow up as they crossed it.

The enemy had by this time come to life and Den Brotheridge, No. 1 Platoon commander, was killed as he led his platoon on the far side of the canal bridge. We were all a bit dazed after the rough landing but acted, after so much training, more or less automatically. There was a good deal too much firing and shouting, which is fairly typical of troops in action for the first time. We cleared the enemy from the slit trenches and dug-outs when I heard the success signals "ham" and "jam" on the radio. John Howard sent for me and, as I made my way to report to him, I was hit in the leg by a burst from a Schmeiser machine pistol, which also hit both my platoon sergeant and my runner. I fell, well and truly *hors de combat*, after what I claim was about twenty-five minutes in action.

The rest is hearsay, but it is worth recording that the third glider landed on our LZ. The platoon commander, Sandy Smith, although wounded, led his platoon across the canal bridge to deal with the expected enemy counter-attack. Two of the three gliders, albeit in the wrong order, landed near the River Orne bridge, which was captured without a shot being fired. The third glider landed on a wrong bridge over the River Dives about 11 Km away. It attacked and captured the bridge, rejoining the Coup de Main party late on D-Day.

Enemy attempts to dislodge the Coup de Main party from the two bridges failed and they were successfully handed over intact to the 7th Battalion Parachute Regiment, who landed early on D-Day.

POSTSCRIPT

The Coup de Main party achieved complete surprise and captured both Pegasus and Horsa Bridges intact, with minimum casualties, within about ten minutes of the initial landing. The fact that the party, despite being one glider short and having another land in the wrong order, was so successful must in no small part be due to the detailed and extensive rehearsals which had been carried out on the Countess Wear bridges, the previous month.

ESCAPE THE HOLOCAUST

KURT WILHELM

Kurt Wilhelm was a Viennese Jew who found refuge in Exeter. His first wife, a fellow Austrian, worked at the bakery in Exwick, but later died of cancer. He later married Etty. His life was clouded by the sadness of his parents' divorce when he was a child, and by the loss of his family. His latter years were unhappy, regretting the absence of children, and fearful of old age. He died in 1989 after a stroke.

I was born in 1906. I was lucky enough to leave Austria through friends. We had our own printing business in Vienna belonging to my grandfather. Through Nazification we lost the business. One day a Nazi came and he said, "This is my business", and threw us out. It was a sort of forced sale... my grandfather had the business in Vienna for over forty years. I was a printer, a compositor, working in Hebrew letters you see. Of course I am talking of old methods of printing when it was all handset.

War hadn't broken out, it was still peace. Things were very, very difficult in Vienna. First we had to scrub floors. They came in the houses and took out the Jews and beat them and we had to scrub the pavement outside. I had to do that. It didn't matter whether you were practising the religion or not, you were a Jew. You were Jewish. You were a "bloody Jew" and that was that. We never practised religion much be we were Jewish. Then you were not allowed to sit in parks anymore. It was only for Aryans. They put signs on the seats "Only Aryans Allowed To Sit Here" just as in South Africa where they write "No Black People".

We had a house there and living in that house we had a housekeeper, she used to be my nanny. When Kristallnacht happened the Nazis, the Blackshirts, the Gestapo, went from house to house, and of course the first thing they asked of the caretaker was were there any Jews living in the house? And he told them - 'There are no Jews here'. We had a four storey house with three Jewish families and he said there were no Jewish people living there. He lied, he defended me.

When I visited Austria again after the war I saw the son of the man who had lied. The old people had died and we came visiting, they gave us a welcome. We stayed in Vienna for a fortnight and they made us very, very welcome. And they all realised what a mistake they had made.

My mother died. She was taken out - that's all I heard from the Red Cross - she was sent to a concentration camp in Poland. I don't even know where. My wife's mother's family they were taken out of bed to a concentration camp. So they all regret very much what happened to us but there are still a lot of Nazis about. They are growing stronger.

My father was in the army during the First World War. He had an Iron Cross. He was an engineer working for the ministry in the war. Oh it devastated us, there was, what shall I say, you went around and you never knew whether you would be alive the next day. During the night they had raids on houses. My mother was living in her own house and all the Jewish people had to go together. They made a sort of place where the Jews had to go together, like a ghetto. And as it was a big house, she used to live in a five bedroom house, they took all the Jews together. And they had a balcony overlooking the garden and there were many that jumped from the balcony and killed themselves. Then we had the Gestapo house - what was going on there we shall never know - people were shouting and crying, looking out of the windows, crying, what's happening to them. The rights of the Jewish people had completely gone.

You see I was lucky to get out. Six million didn't get out. I got nobody. My mother was one of thirteen. All died.

I brought with me to England a machine, a printing machine. Because I had the idea to start on my own one day. The machine came here and I had a job. I was in the British Army then, you see, I was digging trenches in Ilfracombe. I hurst my leg very badly so I was transferred to another company who stayed in the country. So I got in touch with a firm in Exeter. The machine was coming from London to Exeter, but I had no money to pay the duty on it. There was forty pounds duty on it. All that I had wwas fifteen shillings! That was the money I had brought from Austria - you were not allowed to bring money out. The Jews had to give up all their jewellery, gold, silver, cutlery. Everything was collected. They came in the houses and requisitioned it. They gave you a receipt for it, a worthless receipt, not worth a penny. So the machine was in Exeter - unfortunately it didn't work there because it had a different motor. The the blitz came! So I lost the machine - after all that trouble all that I could get was for scrap. So I lost the machine. I lost the idea of working on my own. I lost the chance ever to get established on my own.

But I was full of spirit! We had some bombing raids here and I said, "It's a good job I went out, and my wife went out." Our house was bombed. We were living in Heavitree in those times and I said, "better the machine went than me", because the Heavitree Road wasbadly bombed, where the police station was, was all bombed flat.

I remember old Exeter before the Blitz... vaguely... like a dream. It was a very nice city. But it's all changed...

INDEX